3001 QUESTIONS ALL ABOUT ME

Inspiring | Educating | Creating | Entertaining

Brimming with creative inspiration, how-to projects, and useful information to enrich your everyday life, Quarto Knows is a favorite destination for those pursuing their interests and passions. Visit our site and dig deeper with our books into your area of interest: Quarto Creates, Quarto Cooks, Quarto Homes, Quarto Lives, Quarto Drives, Quarto Explores, Quarto Gifts, or Quarto Kids.

First published in 2020 by Chartwell Books, an imprint of The Quarto Group,
142 West 36th Street, 4th Floor, New York, NY 10018, USA
T (212) 779-4972 F (212) 779-6058 www.QuartoKnows.com

Chartwell titles are also available at discount for retail, wholesale, promotional, and bulk purchase. For details, contact the Special Sales Manager by email at specialsales@quarto.com or by mail at The Quarto Group, Attn: Special Sales Manager, 100 Cummings Center Suite 265D, Beverly, MA 01915 USA.

10 9 8 7 6 5 4 3

ISBN: 978-0-7858-3907-1

Publisher: Rage Kindelsperger
Creative Director: Laura Drew
Managing Editor: Cara Donaldson
Text: Jon Reyes
Cover Design and Interior Design: B. Middleworth

Printed in China TT012021

AM I A GOOD PUBLIC SPEAKER?

WHAT'S MY FAVORITE OUTFIT TO WEAR? • WHAT WAS MY FAVORITE PICTURE BOOK WHEN I WAS A KID?

WHEN I DIE, WHAT DO I WANT MY LEGACY TO BE? • IF I COULD BUY A PIECE OF ART, WHAT WOULD IT BE?

3001 QUESTIONS ALL ABOUT ME

chartwell
books

WHAT'S MY GO-TO KARAOKE SONG?

1. What brings me joy?

2. What kind of noises bother me?

3. Can I describe the first pair of shoes I bought for myself?

4. Have I ever been forgiven? What for?

5. When was the last time I cried? Why?

6. When was the last time I forgave someone? Why?

7. What's my favorite season? Why?

8. How can I become a better listener?

9. What's the best present I've ever received?

10. How do I feel today?

11. When's the last time I went to a hospital? Why?

12. What's my favorite book? Why?

13. What was my first love?

14. Why are the reasons I've fallen in love?

15. How do I like my coffee?

16. How do I like my eggs in the morning?

17. What's my favorite painting?

18. What's my favorite song? Why?

19. Do I remember the first time I was on a plane? What was it like?

20. What was the first election I ever voted in?

21. If I had an imaginary friend as an adult, what would they be like?

22. Who was my first best friend? Do I remember how they met?

23. Do I like or dislike conflict?

24. What's my favorite place on earth?

25. If I could travel anywhere at this moment, where would I go?

26. How would I describe my parents?

27. Have my parents ever embarrassed me?

28. What household appliance would I be able to live without?

29. Who was the person that believed in me?

30. What's the one thing I can control?

31. What do I consider to be a success?

32. What's my biggest failure?

33. When's the last time I went to the doctor?

34. Does a doctor's office scare me?

35. Has anyone ever cried on my shoulder?

36. Have I ever thrown up twice in one night?

37. How regularly do I like to check in with friends?

38. What was my favorite song when I was kid?

39. What's my favorite part about the winter holidays?

40. What's my least favorite part about the winter holidays?

41. What's my biggest fear?

42. What's the thing I'm least afraid of?

43. Have I ever baked a dessert? Should I learn how to?

44. When's the last time I saw a sunset?

45. Do I like to curl up with a good book? Should I do it more often?

46. Do I feel relaxed?

47. What's the worst movie I've ever seen?

48. What's my favorite movie of all-time?

49. What movie can I start watching mid-way through and still enjoy?

50. Do I prefer my hair short or long?

51. What would 10-year-old me say to me right now?

52. Do I like swimming in the ocean, lake, or river?

53. What is my favorite planet?

54. How did I become the person I am today?

55. Who's the person I want to meet most in the world?

56. What's a memory that makes me sad?

57. What's my happiest memory?

58. If I had a catch phrase, what would it be?

59. When's the last time someone said something truly nice to me?

60. Who believed in me when I was young?

61. What do I do in times of crisis?

62. Who deserves my love and affection?

63. Is there someone I could be kinder toward?

64. What was my favorite game while I was growing up?

65. What's my favorite piece of furniture?

66. What is my least favorite piece of furniture?

67. Do I need to fall asleep in total darkness?

68. Am I a light or heavy sleeper?

69. Do I like my eggs scrambled or sunny side up?

70. When I was a kid, what was my favorite thing to eat?

71. When I was a kid, what was my least favorite thing to eat?

72. Who's the funniest person I know? What makes them funny?

73. What's my favorite photograph of myself? What was that day like?

74. What is my least favorite photograph of myself that someone has placed in a picture frame?

75. Have I always hated *that* photo?

76. Who's my favorite singer?

77. Who's my favorite author?

78. What's the one thing I would never do?

79. What's the one thing I would tell people to always do?

80. What kind of parent would I be?

81. What kind of parent do I not want to be?

82. What effect do I have on people?

83. If I could take credit for an invention, which would it be?

84. Have I ever made someone laugh uncontrollably?

85. What's my favorite flower?

86. Have I ever left a party early? Why?

87. What's my earliest memory?

88. Have I ever jumped off a cliff?

89. What was my favorite thing to do in the playground when I was kid?

90. Do I have enemies?

91. Who are my biggest allies?

92. Is there a memory I have with my least favorite food growing up?

93. Am I a good public speaker?

94. What's my go-to karaoke song?

95. What was my favorite picture book when I was a kid?

96. What is my favorite pair of shoes?

97. What's my favorite outfit to wear? Why?

98. When I die, what do I want my legacy to be?

99. If I could buy a piece of art, what would it be?

100. When I was a kid, did I ever have neighbors I really liked?

101. Who was my first crush?

102. Who was my first kiss? What was it like?

103. Would I go to prom today?

104. What's my favorite memory with friends in my 20s?

105. What's my favorite time of day?

106. What's my favorite summer drink?

107. What's the thing I like to do the most when it rains?

108. How much time do I think I've spent apologizing to people?

109. Is there someone who I consider to be unforgivable?

110. Do I believe in the death penalty?

111. Am I a patient person?

112. Have I ever screamed when I was upset?

113. What's my favorite outdoor activity?

114. What's the one thing I do not like to share?

115. Mountain climbing, have I ever done it? Would I ever want to do it?

116. Would I run a marathon?

117. Can I describe my childhood bedroom?

118. What was my favorite TV theme song growing up?

119. What do I picture when I picture myself getting old?

120. Have I ever walked barefoot on a sidewalk? Why?

121. Do I like going to weddings?

122. Is there a wedding I've gone to where I had a lot of fun?

123. Do I believe in marriage?

124. What's my favorite book-turned-into-a-movie?

125. Am I good with power tools?

126. Do I like when people help me? Or am I better off doing things alone?

127. Have I ever felt lonely?

128. When's the last time I called my parents? What did we talk about?

129. What's the last email I sent?

130. What's the last text message I sent?

131. Do I have a favorite Walt Disney film?

132. Do I believe in miracles?

133. Have I ever pretended to like someone?

134. Do I disguise my emotions well?

135. What am I like when I'm sick?

136. Do people think I'm nice or mean?

137. What's my definition of beauty?

138. What's my favorite decade?

139. Do I have a favorite magazine?

140. Do I have a favorite website?

141. Have I ever laughed uncontrollably? Why?

142. What's my favorite poem?

143. What's my definition of paradise?

144. Do I have what it takes to be a teacher?

145. How do I define love?

146. Have I ever prank called someone?

147. Have I ever confessed to something I didn't do? If I haven't, would I?

148. What's my relationship to money?

149. What's my favorite kind of cuisine?

150. If I could make one law, what would it be?

151. If I wrote a memoir, what would the name of it be?

152. Do I remember who taught me how to tie my shoe?

153. What's my best memory of my kindergarten teacher?

154. Have I ever told someone I'm in love with them?

155. Have I ever thought I was in love but then realized I wasn't?

156. Am I a nervous flyer or am I pretty comfortable being in an airplane?

157. Have I ever gone to the movies alone? What was it like? If not, would I do it?

158. Do I have a hobby? If not, what should it be?

159. What's the thing I've always known I could do right?

160. Do I want to learn horseback riding?

161. Who's my best friend? What are they like?

162. What do I love most about my best friend?

163. Do I remember my high school graduation? Was I excited?

164. Am I the type of person that celebrates happy occasions?

165. What was my favorite subject in high school?

166. When I get into a new romantic relationship, what are my boundaries?

167. What's the one thing I've always wanted to learn?

168. Am I good at sports? Do I want to be?

169. What's the one thing that will make me not speak to a person anymore?

170. Am I an overly sensitive person?

171. What's the first thing I notice when I meet someone?

172. Do I care about what people think?

173. What are my three worst habits?

174. What habits do I want to cultivate?

175. If I could learn to cook a specialty dish, who would be the best teacher?

176. Where do I see myself in twenty years?

177. Where do I see myself in five years?

178. Where do I see myself tomorrow?

179. Where do I see myself in ten years?

180. If I could go back in time to speak to a family member, who would it be?

181. What are two things that make me want to give someone a hug?

182. Where do I want to retire?

183. What kind of boss would I be?

184. What kind of boss do I want to be?

185. If I could take one thing with me to a deserted island, what would it be?

186. How do I like to spend my days off?

187. When I go out, how do I like to dress?

188. What's my favorite ice-cream topping?

189. Who's my "in case of emergency?" Why are they the best person to call if there was an emergency?

190. If I could change my name, what would I change it to?

191. If I could go to the jungle, and bring an animal with me as a pet, what animal would it be?

192. If I could buy anything in the world, what would it be?

193. What's the first thing I would give up if my life depended on it?

194. When I feel I've "made it" and become a success?

195. What's my go-to drink at a bar?

196. Do I think someone can be authentic and polite?

197. What are the traits most important to have in a family?

198. Have I meditated recently?

199. Who's the first person I call when something great happens?

200. Who's the first person I can when something bad happens?

201. What's the one smell that reminds me of summer?

202. What's the one smell that reminds me of fall?

203. What's the one smell that reminds me of spring?

204. What's the one smell that reminds me of winter?

205. Who is the most important person in my life?

206. Who do I want to give my eulogy at my funeral?

207. What's the one thing I would not want for the person giving my eulogy to say?

208. When I was a kid, what did I want to be when I grew up?

209. What was the name of my first pet? What were they like?

210. When I wake up, what's the first thing I think about?

211. Who has always held a special place in my heart?

212. What's going to be the biggest challenge of the next generation?

213. When I grow older, what's the story I will repeatedly tell anyone who will listen?

214. Do I have any regrets?

215. What's a scene from my life that I replay over again in my head constantly?

216. Have I ever been seduced?

217. Has anyone called me crazy? Did it offend me?

218. Do I consider myself good at adapting?

219. What kind of spouse do I want to be?

220. What's been the thing that has made me the angriest?

221. Have I ever been wrong?

222. What is the greatest meal I've ever eaten?

223. What are the 5 habits I admire in another person?

224. Who's the most charming person I know?

225. What's the one thing that puts a smile on my face?

226. What was my favorite toy when I was growing up?

227. What's my favorite dish to cook?

228. What was my experience learning to ride a bike?

229. What am I generally grateful for?

230. Have I ever considered shaving my head?

231. Do I prefer roller coasters or Ferris wheels?

232. What was my favorite subject in elementary school?

233. Do I like my boss? Why?

234. Do I like playing in the snow? Why?

235. What's my favorite snack?

236. Have I ever broken up with someone?

237. Have I ever mentored someone? Would I want to?

238. Who's the last person I had dinner with? What was it like?

239. If I could donate a million dollars to any charity which would I give the money to?

240. If I could insert myself as the star of one of my favorite movies which would it be?

241. Can I recite my favorite poem from memory and write it down?

242. What's the first thing I do when I am unplugged?

243. What's my favorite TV show right now?

244. If I were told that I have one more hug to give in my entire life, who would I give it to?

245. What's one giveaway to people around me that I am happy?

246. Would I sell my pet for a one million dollars?

247. If I could go on TV and interview anyone, who would it be?

248. If I could only have one photograph on my mantle, which would it be?

249. What's the craziest thing I've seen on the street?

250. Do I feel like my life is moving forward or backward?

251. Is there a goal I've put off in accomplishing?

252. Am I scared of shots at the doctor's office?

253. Am I afraid of the dark?

254. How did I sleep last night?

255. Have I ever wanted to ask a question but know that I wouldn't like the answer?

256. What do I love learning about?

257. What's the best road trip I've ever been on?

258. What do I feel is good in my life?

259. What do I need to do today?

260. What question do I always ask without hesitation?

261. Is there anything I'd rather be doing during my free time?

262. What's the most embarrassing thing I've ever lived through?

263. What's the worst argument I've ever been in?

264. Is someone ignoring me? How do I feel about it?

265. What do I feel the world needs?

266. What part of my life am I trying to keep a secret from people?

267. What can't I bring myself to believe?

268. What's my favorite day of the week?

269. Have I ever cried over spilt milk?

270. Did I have a big imagination as a child?

271. What's the best holiday I ever had?

272. Do I like long walks?

273. What's the best thing I have ever made?

274. How do I tend to comfort people?

275. What's the last thing I learned that blew me away?

276. What's the best feedback I've ever received?

277. When am I the best version of myself? In the morning, afternoon, or night?

278. How do I let my significant other know I care about them?

279. How do I like those in my life to be affectionate?

280. What do I believe will never happen?

281. If I could only say one phrase in my life, which would it be?

282. Do I like going to the beach? Why?

283. Who are the people I always ask for advice?

284. What was my favorite candy growing up? Is there a memory attached to it?

285. What is my favorite pizza topping?

286. When I was a kid, who was my favorite relative?

287. What's the one thing I always did on Saturday mornings when I was kid?

288. What do I think about when I look at my parents?

289. When I look outside my window, what do I see?

290. What can I do to help the state of the world?

291. What's my least favorite color?

292. Do I know the story of the day I was born?

293. What's my least favorite smell?

294. What am I most confident in when it comes to who I am?

295. If I had to describe myself in one word, which would it be?

296. What do I answer when someone asks me to tell them about myself?

297. As I grow older, what's the one thing I want to keep with me?

298. What was it like the first time I went to a bar?

299. Is there a mystery I would like to solve?

300. What's the last thing I read that I can't wait to tell people about?

301. What's the first job I ever got paid for?

302. How much was my first paycheck for?

303. Who is on the top of my guest list for my next birthday celebration?

304. What do I consider to be a good marriage?

305. Who do I consider to be a living angel?

306. Have I ever been called bossy? How did that make me feel?

307. Do I sleep with the door open or closed?

308. Have I ever been in a bad accident?

309. Have I ever been depressed?

310. Have I ever been the bad guy?

311. Have I ever lost a pet? What's my best memory of them?

312. How do I reward myself?

313. What do I feel when I hear a recording of my own voice?

314. What's my favorite thing about being in a car?

315. Have I ever broken a promise?

316. Have I ever won a competition?

317. Have I ever jumped for joy?

318. What's the story I've told over and over again?

319. How do I view time?

320. What's the sweetest thing anyone has ever done for me?

321. Who have I told my biggest secret to?

322. Who have I disappointed?

323. What's my favorite movie genre?

324. What's my favorite beverage?

325. Why do/don't I keep a planner?

326. What would surprise people to hear about me?

327. What's the worst typo I've ever typed?

328. Have I ever been in a physical fight?

329. Have I ever been ashamed of something?

330. Could I be a politician?

331. Who do I think about a lot?

332. Do I hold grudges easily?

333. Do I judge people easily?

334. Am I a competitive person?

335. When's the last time I took a deep breath?

336. When will I be the person I set out to be?

337. Have I ever learned a shocking secret about someone?

338. Who do I think is the most dangerous person in the world?

339. Have I ever borrowed something and never returned it?

340. Have I ever told someone they are good at something and I didn't believe it?

341. What's my favorite thing in a coffee shop?

342. If I were to write a novel, what would it be about?

343. Who would I want to bring with me to a deserted island?

344. What's the scariest movie I've ever seen?

345. Has someone ever interrogated me?

346. Who taught me how to cook?

347. What's the best first impression I've ever made?

348. Have I ever been kind to a stranger?

349. When am I the most tired?

350. Why am I doing this?

351. What is the first thing that comes to mind when I hear "kindness"?

352. If I could move anywhere, where would I move?

353. Have I bought flowers for someone?

354. Have I ever opened the door for someone?

355. What's the longest I've gone without speaking to someone?

356. How do I feel when I see old video footage of myself?

357. If I were asked to be on a reality show, would I say yes?

358. What's my morning wake-up routine?

359. When will I be able to say what I want?

360. What does my dream house look like?

361. If I could go on any adventure, what would I choose?

362. Do I need to speak up more?

363. If there was a list called "New Me," what would I add to it?

364. What makes me lose my concentration?

365. Am I addicted to my cell phone?

366. Do I judge people who are addicted to their cell phone?

367. Why did I wear the clothes I'm wearing today?

368. If I had a superpower, what would it be? Why?

369. If I could host one game show, which would it be?

370. What's my favorite spot where I live?

371. Have I ever skinny-dipped? Would I?

372. What is all I need?

373. How do I ensure I never forget who I am?

374. What do I consider to be a good life?

375. Who have I met that I consider mysterious?

376. What do I love most about my body?

377. What do I like least about my body? Why?

378. Do I like to dance?

379. If I could speak one more language, which would it be?

380. How would I pass the days in tranquility?

381. Have I ever screamed at someone?

382. How do I make sure I remember the good times I've had with old friends?

383. What's the thing I've always wanted to dream about while I sleep and never have?

384. What's the wildest thing I've ever done?

385. What's something I've done that I thought was wild, but really wasn't?

386. What's the most bizarre thing I've ever done for money?

387. Who have I seen bloom into an amazing person?

388. Have I made someone cry but never meant to?

389. Have I ever promised someone I will never let them down?

390. Have I ever been suspicious of someone?

391. If I didn't have love for those around me, what would it be like?

392. Do I like having leftovers?

393. Have I ever wanted to do something and have been stopped?

394. Do I know how to play chess? Do I like playing? If not, do I want to learn?

395. Have I ever physically run away from something?

396. Have I ever physically run away from someone?

397. Do I have a fear of dying young?

398. When I hear birds singing, what do I think about?

399. Do I believe in God?

400. Do I believe in religion?

401. How often do I stop to breathe?

402. Have I ever skipped going to bed? Why?

403. Has there been someone who has left my life and I feel great about it?

404. When was the last time I rested?

405. When was the last time I physically called on someone?

406. Have I ever chain smoked?

407. When's the last time I felt 100% alive?

408. How many times has someone lied to me?

409. Do I like being around animals?

410. Who is the one person that has changed my life?

411. Do I like change?

412. Have I ever chased someone?

413. Have I ever chased something?

414. Has anyone ever told me they were going to teach me something?

415. Who's the most toxic person in my life?

416. What do I think about when I look at a clock?

417. What's the main thing that I consider to be my prerogative?

418. Who do I know that always looks good?

419. What am I most grateful for today?

420. Have I ever told someone something that was supposed to be a secret?

421. Do I consider myself to be trustworthy?

422. Has a song ever made me cry? Why?

423. Do I think every time I fall in love will be like the first time?

424. Have I ever dreamed the same dream several nights in a row?

425. Do I tend to focus on the same thing?

426. What do I know for sure?

427. Has there been a moment for me where I have vowed something?

428. Who possesses the right qualities to change the world?

429. If I really wanted to do something today, could someone stop me?

430. Is there something I want to do today? Could someone stop me?

431. What's a horror movie that always scares me?

432. Do I believe all people have a soul?

433. If someone asked me for shelter, would I give it to them?

434. Have I ever tried to take something from someone?

435. Does my name define me?

436. What do I have unwavering faith in?

437. If I were to devote myself to something, what would it be?

438. Do I live for something?

439. Do I feel courageous today?

440. What's the one thing that I could accomplish that would make me feel like I don't need to accomplish anymore?

441. Do I like my life at home?

442. Who do I trust the most?

443. Who has the prettiest eyes of everyone I know?

444. If I could dance like anyone, who would it be?

445. If I could be born in another era, which would I pick?

446. Have I ever been in love but then realized I was just "in like"?

447. What do I deserve?

448. What's the one thing I've always wanted?

449. Have I ever asked someone not to speak? Who was it?

450. Have I ever given someone an ultimatum?

451. Have I ever been soaked by a rainstorm? Was it fun?

452. Did I ever believe in the tooth fairy?

453. Has there ever been a night where all I wanted to do was go out and hang out with friends?

454. Have I ever asked myself, "What if?"

455. Do I consider myself a transparent person?

456. Has anyone ever dropped a figurative bomb in my life?

457. Do I think I ever lived a past life?

458. When have I ever gone against the grain?

459. What's the one thing I want to live to tell?

460. What have I lived and learned?

461. Have I ever been in a blackout? What was it like?

462. What's my favorite memory of playing outside when I was kid?

463. How do I define sensuality?

464. What's the one thing I cannot get enough of?

465. Do I believe in therapy?

466. What is the best night of my life?

467. Have I ever walked away from something or someone because it wasn't right for me?

468. Have I ever mistakenly given someone the wrong impression?

469. What's the best feeling in the world?

470. What have I left behind?

471. What's the one vision I've had that has come true?

472. What's been the best year of my life?

473. Have I ever wanted to be the most important person to someone? Why?

474. What impresses me the most from a travel destination?

475. What impresses me the least from a travel destination?

476. What impresses me the most from a person?

477. What impresses me the least from a person?

478. Am I a romantic?

479. Am I a realist?

480. What possession do I cherish the most?

481. Have I ever heard something that has left me speechless?

482. Who is the only person that makes me feel better?

483. If the day had 25 hours, what would I use that extra hour for?

484. What are the kinds of moments I tend to recall easily?

485. Who do I want to give a kiss to today?

486. Have I ever been the recipient of hand-me-downs? What did it feel like?

487. What's the one feeling that can't be beat?

488. What process do I enjoy most?

489. Have I ever told someone they need to wait their turn? How did I feel when I did?

490. Do I think charisma is a quality or a skill?

491. Underneath it all, do I think the person who gives me the hardest time likes me?

492. Do I believe in "the one"?

493. Has there been a moment where I told myself to hold on?

494. What's the one thing I believe no one can hold inside?

495. Who is the most irresponsible person I know?

496. If I could say I'm sorry to someone, who would it be? Why?

497. Who was the last person that kept me waiting? How did that make me feel?

498. Do I have a favorite city?

499. Do I know someone who makes me feel confident every time I interact with them?

500. Do I think eyeglasses make someone look cool?

501. Does getting older scare me?

502. Has there been a time in my life where many things changed rapidly? How did that make me feel?

503. What's the easiest thing I've ever done?

504. Have I uttered the words, "Maybe you're right"?

505. When I stand in front of a mirror, what do I see?

506. What are three grievances I have today?

507. Who has broken my heart?

508. Has someone ever scared me?

509. What do I do every Sunday morning?

510. If I were given the choice to live forever, would I do it?

511. Do I pray? Why?

512. What would I do to survive in a desert?

513. Do I get sad when it rains? Why?

514. What's my favorite board game?

515. What's the worst board game to ever exist?

516. What do I remember about my favorite teacher?

517. Who have I missed the most?

518. Do I believe in luck?

519. What do I do to quell my anxiety?

520. Who was my first slow dance with?

521. Do I believe in heaven?

522. Do I believe in hell?

523. When have I felt the most lost?

524. If I could build a house anywhere would I do it on a tropical island

or in the middle of a forest?

525. What is the one thing I believe can only be done one way?

526. What is the one thing I believe can be done in a variety of ways
for the same outcome?

527. How would I want to talk about the love of my life?

528. Who makes me feel good when I spend quality time with them?

529. Do I know how to change a diaper? If so, how did I learn? If not, do I need to learn?

530. What's the one thing I've always wanted to say?

531. Who's a bad influence in my life?

532. Who's a good influence in my life?

533. What are 5 bad habits I hate seeing in other people?

534. Am I bad at love?

535. Am I good at love?

536. What kind of person am I when I am single?

537. What kind of person am I when I am romantically involved?

538. Have I ever asked someone to leave my home? What would make me do that?

539. Has someone ever asked me to leave their home? Why?

540. Was I a mischievous kid?

541. What's my favorite musical genre?

542. What's my least favorite musical genre? Why?

543. What am I most proud of?

544. What am I least proud of?

545. If I could use a "Do Not Disturb" sign at any moment, when would I use it?

546. What has happened to me that has made me think, "Wow, I'm really lucky"?

547. Have I ever declared ownership of something? Did it belong to me?

548. Has anyone ever taken credit for an idea of mine?

549. If I could heal a physical or emotional injury for someone else, what would it be?

550. Have I ever taken back an invite? Why?

551. What's the first thing I ask for when I get to a restaurant?

552. What's the last thing I want to ask for when I am at a restaurant?

553. Have I ever wanted to protect someone?

554. What keeps me up at night?

555. What song always reminds me of someone?

556. Did I ever learn something and then wished I never learned it?

557. Have I ever wasted someone's time?

558. What is something I've broken that I wish I could put back together?

559. What's the one thing I never wanted to share as a child?

560. If I only had one dollar, what would I do with it?

561. What do most people consider bad that I don't?

562. What's the worst idea I've ever had?

563. Did I ever throw something out and then regret it?

564. What inspires me to be daring?

565. What do I need right now?

566. Have I ever done something bad?

567. What's the one thing I would want for myself in the next life?

568. Am I a good liar?

569. Is there a day I think about often?

570. Have I ever complimented someone? What did I say?

571. Who should I compliment?

572. What's the one thing I think should be forever?

573. If I could sell something today, what would I sell?

574. Am I lonely?

575. Is there a difference between being alone and feeling lonely?

576. Is there a moment in my life I wish I would have paid more attention during?

577. What is the one thing that I know won't ever come back when it leaves?

578. Have I ever been paranoid? Why?

579. What's the deepest conversation I've ever had with a stranger?

580. What's the deepest conversation I've ever had with a family member?

581. If I could eradicate one thing from earth, what would it be?

582. What would I like to have written on my tombstone?

583. What's the most ordinary thing about me?

584. What's the most extraordinary thing about me?

585. Have I ever loved someone for the wrong reasons?

586. If I could make something in my life automatic, what would it be?

587. What's the most beautiful thing I've seen today?

588. If I could lend someone a hand, who would it be?

589. Have I ever not helped someone in need?

590. Do I look forward to the future?

591. Who do I know that gives the best hugs?

592. Who is the one person I would never make a promise to?

593. Do I like cold or room temperature water?

594. What's the most fun party I've ever been to?

595. Have I ever realized later on that someone was right?

596. What's the most significant moment in my life?

597. What do most people want that I don't?

598. Have I ever had an outer body experience?

599. What's the lowest I've been in my life?

600. What's my anthem?

601. Has there been a time I've known exactly what I needed to do?

602. What's the one thing I believe no one can ever rush?

603. If I could eliminate one thing from my life, what would it be?

604. When have I felt the readiest?

605. Who do I know really well?

606. What do I know really well?

607. When am I at 100%?

608. Do I believe things are getting better?

609. What do I trust the most?

610. How do I change the tone of a conversation?

611. What's the hardest thing I've ever done?

612. Do I gossip a lot?

613. What makes me automatically want to be friends with someone?

614. Has the last person that hugged me really tight?

615. Are teachers important to me?

616. Has someone ever claimed I didn't love them enough?

617. Who do I wish I still spoke to?

618. Have you ever hidden from someone?

619. If I could give praise to someone I've never met, who would it be?

620. What's my favorite memory from kindergarten?

621. Have I ever envied someone?

622. Do I believe people fall in love at the same time?

623. How do I internally check-in with myself every day?

624. What is the one thing I never talk about when meeting someone for the first time?

625. If I could go back and start something again, what would it be?

626. Have I ever been in a codependent relationship?

627. Do I think there's something I can do that no one else can?

628. Where does compassion begin for me?

629. Do I believe an older person is always wise?

630. Who do I hate for knowing me so well?

631. If I could be a native from somewhere else in the world, where would it be?

632. Is fidelity a feeling or a decision?

633. Have you ever waved at someone that ended up not being the person you thought they were originally? Did that embarrass you?

634. What do I consider to be no one's business?

635. What is freedom to me?

636. What has been the most beautiful surprise in my life?

637. What instrumental sound do I hear and immediately feel relaxed?

638. When's the last time I applied pressure on myself? How did that go?

639. Has anyone ever cried over me?

640. Who do I know that has not changed? Is that a good thing?

641. Have I ever had a breakthrough?

642. What have I done so far today? Is that enough?

643. What's the one part of me that I cannot die?

644. Do I have a green thumb?

645. When am I most resilient?

646. Have I ever willed myself not to cry?

647. What's the one thing I will always say yes to?

648. Why am I unique?

649. If I had to be handcuffed to someone for a day, who would I pick to be handcuffed with me?

650. Today I have the strength to admit something, what is it?

651. What do I think is one of my biggest faults?

652. What happens when I get bored?

653. If I won a million dollars, what is the first thing I do?

654. If I could fly anywhere, where would I want to go?

655. Would I survive on a deserted island?

656. Who has an ability that I trust?

657. Am I able to turn my emotions on or off?

658. What about me would make someone write a movie about my life?

659. Am I above asking someone for help when it is really needed?

660. What is the one thing I've accepted from someone that I never should?

661. What would be the first sentence in a book titled *Life According to Me?*

662. When I make decisions that involve others do, I account for how I feel?

663. Do I know someone who comes across as too-good-to-be-true?

664. Have I ever encountered someone who can act really well?

665. What's the one action I could take today to make me happy?

666. What's my favorite family activity?

667. Have I ever actualized a dream into existence?

668. What's the one thing I could add to my life today to make it better?

669. Have I ever listened to a speech and thought I would want to be the one giving it?

670. What's the worst experience I've had at the DMV?

671. Has anyone ever admitted to me they had a crush on me a long time ago?

672. When I was a child, did I ever think I would be the kind of adult I am today?

673. How do my decisions affect others?

674. After I retire, what do I want people to say about me at work?

675. If I could go on a trip again, which would it be?

676. Has anyone ever been against an idea I had? How did that make me feel?

677. Do I believe there's a specific age one can do things?

678. If I could start my own business what would it be?

679. How can I be an agent of change?

680. How long ago was the last time I told someone they mean a lot to me?

681. Do I agree with most of the people around me?

682. Is there an unspoken agreement with people around me that I will go along with what they decide?

683. What am I looking forward to?

684. When was the last time I went outside to get some air?

685. If I could give someone all the money in the world, who would I give it to?

686. Do I allow people around me to get away with things I wouldn't let myself get away with?

687. What is the last thing I almost did?

688. If I could be alone today, what would I do?

689. Who do I get along with all the time?

690. When's the last time someone asked me to do something I had already done? How did that make me feel?

691. Who was the last person who inspired me to do something?

692. Has anyone ever made me angry even though I wanted to laugh at that moment?

693. What's the one thing that someone can always count on me for?

694. What do I say to myself when I am frustrated?

695. Do I consider myself among the funniest people I know?

696. What amount of money would make me quit my job?

697. If I could put together an analysis on any person on earth, who would it be?

698. Have I ever improvised something?

699. What's my favorite animal?

700. What's another way I could approach conflict?

701. What would be a funny answer to the last serious question someone asked me?

702. Are there any other professions I would go into?

703. Does anyone in this world understand me?

704. Is there anything I would never do?

705. Has someone who passed ever appeared in my dreams?

706. What job would I apply to at this very moment if nothing was stopping me?

707. Has someone ever approached me to help me and I thought they were a threat? Why?

708. Is there an area in my life I would like to totally revamp?

709. Do I like to argue?

710. If I had to get a tattoo on my arm, what would I get?

711. Who's always around me? Do I want them to be?

712. Do I know someone who always arrives late? How does that make me feel?

713. What do I consider to be the best art?

714. Is there an article of clothing I think the world should abolish?

715. Do I have a favorite artist? Why are they my favorite?

716. As someone's best friend, what rights do I have?

717. I'm going to ask someone a good question today, what will it be?

718. Have I ever assumed something about someone and was totally wrong?

719. At what point in my life will I become wise?

720. Have I ever attacked someone? Has someone ever attacked me? How did it feel?

721. What do I always pay attention to when I'm in a new place?

722. If I were an attorney, who would I defend?

723. Have I ever pictured an audience naked when I was speaking in public?

724. If I was an author what kind of stories would I be known for?

725. Who has total authority over my life?

726. Am I available to the closest people in my life?

727. What do I always avoid?

728. When I am away from those I love, do I always miss them?

729. When I was a baby, what was I like?

730. Has anyone ever stabbed me in the back?

731. What is the one bad thing I would eliminate from the world?

732. If I always had to carry a bag what would be in it?

733. When was the last time someone threw a ball at me? What was I doing?

734. What's the one thing I always save?

735. Do I have a favorite chocolate bar?

736. If my life were a baseball game, what base am I on today?

737. If I could be anyone else, who would I be?

738. Who's the last person to beat me at a game? How did it make me feel?

739. Who is the most beautiful person in the world?

740. Have I seen someone suffer because of something someone else has said?

741. Has anyone I know become a different person, and I've told them?

742. Do I like my bed?

743. Can I reference my life in terms of before something and after something? What was that something?

744. If someone asked me about my life, where do I begin my story?

745. What do I consider to be unacceptable behavior?

746. What is something that I've put behind me? Why?

747. Is there someone I will always believe?

748. Have I ever benefited from someone's misfortunes? How did that make me feel?

749. What is the best way to deliver bad news to someone?

750. Am I a better person than I was last year?

751. Am I a better person than I was five years ago?

752. Am I a better person than I was ten years ago?

753. Have I ever had to choose between two people? How did that make me feel? How did I make that decision?

754. What's beyond my control?

755. What do I consider to be a big inconvenience?

756. What do I consider to be a small inconvenience?

757. If I could be known for turning a bill into a law, what would it be?

758. If I had a billion dollars, what would I do differently than if I had a million dollars?

759. If someone asked me to show them a bit of my life, what would I show them?

760. Do I believe in the world in terms of black and white?

761. Have I ever given blood? Why?

762. When was the last time I noticed a clear blue sky?

763. If I were a company, who would be on my board of directors?

764. Who has a body I admire? What do I admire about it?

765. If someone asked me what the last book I read was, what would I tell them?

766. Do I believe we are born with a set destiny, or do we have the power to change it?

767. Have I ever wanted two things? What would have happened had I gotten the chance to have both?

768. What would I put in a box that needed to define my life?

769. What is something boys should learn from a very young age?

770. If I could break something today, what would I choose? Why?

771. If I could bring two people together, who would they be?

772. What makes a good brother?

773. Have I ever made a budget for myself? Did I follow it?

774. What is the one thing I want to build from scratch?

775. Have I ever walked past a building and admired it?

776. What is good business?

777. Has there been something that I've never wanted to do but have always encouraged to do?

778. What's the last thing I bought? Did I need it or want it? Why?

779. What's the one thing I can always stand by?

780. Who is the last person I called? What was the conversation like?

781. Do I like the camera? Why?

782. Have I ever campaigned for something? Do I want to?

783. Can I let someone I know exactly what I think? Who is that person?

784. Is there something that has gotten bigger in my life? Is that a good thing or bad thing?

785. What do I do when I have to make a choice? Do I write things down? Do I talk to someone?

786. If I could change the capital of my country, which city would I choose? Why?

787. Can I describe my first car?

788. What's the last message I wrote in a birthday card? Did I mean it?

789. Who has cared the most about me in my life?

790. Is a career important?

791. Do I carry a lot with me when I travel? Why?

792. If I had to plead my case for wanting something, what's my approach?

793. Do I consider myself a catch?

794. What causes me to be indifferent toward someone or something?

795. What is a basic item in my life I always need?

796. What's the center of my world?

797. What do I consider to be a cardinal truth?

798. What do I wish the human race could accomplish in this century?

799. Have I ever seen someone be certain about something and be totally wrong?

800. What can the world do without?

801. If I could have anyone in the world sit across from me at this very moment, who would it be?

802. What's a challenge I want to overcome?

803. Have I ever taken a chance in my life? How did I feel?

804. Do I want to change someone? Why?

805. What kind of character do I tend to like when I'm reading a story?

806. Who would I put in charge of the world if it had to be one person?

807. Who do I check-in with regularly? Why?

808. What would I tell myself as a child? Why?

809. Do I believe having choices always helps people?

810. If I had to choose between living in a city or a rural area forever, what would I choose? Why?

811. When's the last time I went to a church? What was it like?

812. Do I believe we are citizens of the world?

813. Do big crowds make me nervous?

814. What do I consider to be civil discourse? Is it helpful?

815. If I could claim a catchphrase that already exists, which would it be?

816. What was my favorite class growing up?

817. How can I be clearer when communicating with others?

818. Has there been a moment I saw something clearly?

819. How do I close a chapter in my life?

820. What kind of coach would I be?

821. When's the last time I had a cold? What was it like?

822. If I could put together a collection of knick-knacks, what would it have?

823. Is college important?

824. If my day was a color which would it be? Why?

825. Who was the last person that moved away?

826. Has a TV commercial ever made me cry? Which one?

827. What do I believe is a common human trait?

828. How can I describe my community in one word?

829. Who is always good company?

830. Do I compare people regularly?

831. What's the last thing I did on my computer? Why was it important?

832. What causes me to become concerned about something?

833. What's the one condition I need to have met when I welcome something new in my life?

834. What happened the last time I was in a conference room?

835. What do I remember about the last time I voted for something?

836. What should everyone consider when they make a decision?

837. How often do I think about what I'm watching on TV?

838. Have I ever stuttered? Why?

839. What is the one way I can continue being a better person?

840. Have I ever had control over something?

841. What is the real cost of someone's freedom?

842. What is the one thing that could change the life of those closest to me?

843. Am I a patriotic person?

844. Who is the best couple I know?

845. What do I believe would change the course of a person's life?

846. How much influence does someone's opinion have on me?

847. Have I ever covered something up?

848. If I could create something that would change the word, what would it be?

849. What do I believe is the ultimate punishment?

850. Have I ever wanted to create my own cultural customs?

851. What is my culture?

852. Is my cup half full or half empty?

853. How do I feel about the current state of the world today?

854. Is the customer always right?

855. Is there someone I've thought about cutting out of my life?

856. What advice would I give someone in the darkest time of their life?

857. Is there information I can always recall very quickly?

858. What do I want my future daughter to be like?

859. Could I describe what I would want an exciting day to be like?

860. Is there anyone dead or alive who I would want to be part of my family?

861. What's the best deal I've ever made?

862. What's the worst deal I've ever made?

863. Has there been a death that has affected me?

864. Is there anyone I would like to debate?

865. What's my favorite decade?

866. Who decides what kind of world we live in?

867. Have I ever helped someone make a decision? How did I do that?

868. Does swimming in the deep end of a pool scare me?

869. What is the worst defense anyone could ever use after wronging another human being?

870. What degree of caution should someone always practice?

871. How would I describe the worst day?

872. How would I describe the best day?

873. Has someone ever asked me to describe them? Did I do a good job?

874. If I could redesign something, what would it be?

875. What would make me cheer for someone despite themselves?

876. What is the one detail I always remember about my day?

877. How do I determine if someone says they need something but they really just want it?

878. How do I develop a better relationship with my parents?

879. How do I want to evolve professionally?

880. If I die today, have I done everything I wanted to do?

881. What's the difference between someone hearing me and listening to me?

882. What's different about the person I care about the most since I met them?

883. Do I know someone who is very difficult?

884. What am I making for dinner today? Why?

885. Is there a direction I want my life to go?

886. If I was a movie director what's the one thing I would always tell an actor?

887. When I discover something, what do I always tend to do?

888. Who do I want to discuss my love life with? Why?

889. What's the one discussion I don't want to have today?

890. Is there a disease that plagues the human race that isn't considered a disease?

891. What do I do successfully?

892. Have I ever had a favorite doctor? Why?

893. Am I a dog person?

894. Is it true that when one door closes another opens? When has that happened to me?

895. Is it true that what goes up must come down? When have I ever seen that happen?

896. If I could draw at this very moment, what would I choose to draw?

897. Has someone ever described a crazy dream to me?

898. Can I describe what I see when I look to my left?

899. If I could drive anywhere, where would I drive?

900. When was the last time I dropped something on the floor? How did that make me feel?

901. Have I ever done drugs? Why?

902. Do I think about something during every human interaction?

903. If I could give someone a gift each time they make me happy, who would I choose?

904. What's the earliest I've ever woken up? Why?

905. What's the latest I've ever woken up? Why?

906. Do I have a good sense of direction?

907. Do things come easy to me?

908. What do I want to eat right now?

909. What's the last thing I want to eat right now?

910. What's my relationship with money?

911. What's my relationship with food?

912. What brings me to the edge of madness?

913. Do I think education can change the world?

914. What effect does music have on me?

915. If I could make a better effort in something today, what should it be?

916. What do I think about when I think about the number eight?

917. Between spending time with my friends or spending time with family, which of those makes me feel the best?

918. Have I ever turned someone down? Why?

919. Is there anything else I should do today?

920. Has someone ever hired me to do something I didn't want to do?

921. Is there an ending of a movie I wish I could change?

922. What is the most perfect ending to a movie?

923. Is someone's energy contagious, or no?

924. What is the one thing I've always been immune to?

925. What have I enjoyed today?

926. Can I ever have enough of something?

927. Who is the last person that entered a room I was in? Can I describe them?

928. Who in the entire world would make a great meal for me?

929. Do I care about the environment?

930. If I were allowed to kiss anyone at the moment, who would it be?

931. Who is especially mean when they are hungry?

932. How do I establish a great connection with someone?

933. Do I believe all relationships should be even?

934. Can I describe the perfect evening?

935. What is my favorite annual event?

936. Do I believe in happily ever after?

937. Every person should own this one thing. What is it?

938. Do I believe everybody should be a parent?

939. Does everyone need a good sense of humor?

940. What do I consider to be my everything?

941. What is the evidence that someone has left an impression on your life?

942. What exactly makes a good parent?

943. Who is the best example of what to always do?

944. What kind of executive authority would I give the last person I had an interaction with?

945. What do I wish existed?

946. Do I expect a lot from those closest to me?

947. What experience should every person have by the age of ten?

948. If I could be an expert on something, what would it be?

949. How would I explain the birds and the bees to a child?

950. Do I wish I could change the color of my eyes? Why?

951. What's the best feature on my face?

952. What is an indisputable fact in my life?

953. What should a leader factor in when they make a decision that has to do with people they are leading?

954. What's the last failure I witnessed?

955. When's the last time I fell?

956. Does my family support me?

957. How far is too far?

958. Do I like fast food?

959. What makes a good father?

960. Is fear important?

961. What makes me feel motivated?

962. Is there a feeling I wish I could eliminate?

963. What are the few things I can do to help someone today?

964. What's in my current field of view?

965. What's the last fight I witnessed?

966. Does how I feel figure prominently in how nice I am to someone? Would they notice if I didn't?

967. If I could fill-in for any job in the world, which would it be?

968. What's the last film that made me cry?

969. Did I ever take a final test that made me really nervous? What was going on?

970. If there was finally a way to prevent people from dying, what's the first thing I would do?

971. Does someone's financial standing have a lot to do with them as a person?

972. Is there a missing person I wish I could find?

973. Who would I call a fine person?

974. Has someone ever pointed their finger at me? How did that make me feel?

975. When I finish a book, what do I do right afterward?

976. When's the last time I saw a fire? What was happening?

977. Does someone I know have a firm belief in something I don't agree with? How do I deal with that?

978. Who was the first person to tell me I was special?

979. Have I ever gone fishing? Do I want to? What do I imagine it to be like?

980. If I could name the top five qualities in a friend, what would they be?

981. What's the highest floor I would live in?

982. If someone volunteered to teach me how to fly a plane, would I accept?

983. Is there something I should be focusing on?

984. Who would I follow unconditionally?

985. Should food be unlimited?

986. How do I make sure I put my best foot forward at the beginning of the day?

987. Who is this for?

988. When I'm forced to do something, what do I tell myself?

989. Have I ever wanted to be a foreign exchange student? Why?

990. What do I always forget?

991. What's my least favorite question in a form I have to fill out?

992. What's something I tried once that I will not try again?

993. Should I always make sure I have something to look forward to?

994. What are the four most important books everyone should read?

995. Do I believe I have free choice?

996. Would anyone ever be a friend and at the same time be a foe?

997. From one to ten, how would I rate the last meal I had? Why?

998. What is a full life?

999. If I had the money, what would I fund indefinitely?

1000. What do I want my future to hold?

1001. What's the last game I won?

1002. What are the five vegetables I would grow if I had a garden, and why?

1003. If I could turn any material that exists in abundance into car gas, what would it be?

1004. What kind of humor am I generally comfortable with?

1005. What defines my generation?

1006. What should every girl experience by the time they are ten years old?

1007. What should all people give one another?

1008. When's the last time I saw glass break? What was happening?

1009. When I go somewhere new, I always do this. What is it?

1010. What's a goal everyone should have, even if they don't accomplish it?

1011. What makes a good meal?

1012. What makes someone a great person?

1013. Has someone ever described me as "green"? Did that offend me?

1014. What keeps me grounded?

1015. What person am I when I'm in a group? Am I the funny one?
The inquisitive one? The observer?

1016. How do I grow my spiritual capital?

1017. How do I define personal growth?

1018. Do I believe in owning a gun?

1019. What makes someone a good guy?

1020. How much does someone's hairstyle define them?

1021. Is giving someone half of what I own a tall order?

1022. Who gave me a helping hand when I was a high school student? What do I remember about it?

1023. Who am I always open to hang with?

1024. What happened the last time I decided to have fun?

1025. Who is the happiest person I know?

1026. How hard do I think it is to make changes in my life?

1027. Do I believe that when people have what they want, they don't try anymore?

1028. Who do I know that I would describe as having a good head on their shoulders?

1029. Do I value my health? How do I value it?

1030. When I hear someone laughing, what do I think about?

1031. How do I make sure I t ake care of someone else's heart?

1032. Do I like the heat?

1033. Has there been an instance where I've made a decision to not have a heavy talk with someone? Why?

1034. Do I ask for help when I need it?

1035. Do I believe I was always meant to be here?

1036. What's high on my list of things to consider when I move somewhere?

1037. What's a part of history we collectively tend to forget but should be thinking about often?

1038. Has anyone ever hit on me? What was it like?

1039. What's the longest I've been on hold for?

1040. How do I define a home?

1041. Do I tap into hope often?

1042. What do I hate about hospitals?

1043. Who would I consider to be hot?

1044. What was the last time I stayed at a hotel? Do I enjoy hotel stays?

1045. Do I measure my days in hours or minutes?

1046. What is the last time I saw a house that took my breath away?

1047. What's the most important question? What? How? Or why?

1048. How does someone create a huge impression?

1049. What do I believe is the best thing about being human?

1050. When's the last time someone gave me a hundred-dollar bill?

1051. Who do I know that is the best husband?

1052. What do I usually do when someone is rude to me?

1053. What's my favorite million-dollar idea?

1054. How do I identify myself to the world?

1055. If I were someone in a position of power, what would I do differently?

1056. If I could paint an image in my mind, which would it be?

1057. When I imagine a perfect world, what do I see?

1058. Do I believe that when someone has a great impact and knows it, they are always mindful of people's feelings?

1059. What's important to me today?

1060. What do I believe is the main indicator that someone has improved on something?

1061. What's in a name?

1062. What is the most important quality to include when you're thinking of bringing something to your team?

1063. Do I believe there is an increase of cruelty in the world?

1064. What do I believe is the way to indicate to someone how I feel?

1065. What makes an individual stand out?

1066. What information is vital for someone to know when they want to marry someone?

1067. I believe this exists in every person, what is it?

1068. What should I be doing instead of what I am doing now?

1069. Is there an institution I believe in? Which one?

1070. What always interests me?

1071. Do I like interviews?

1072. What was I into when I was kid?

1073. If I could make an investment, what would I invest in?

1074. What is the one thing I believe love should always involve?

1075. What do I believe are my deep-seated issues?

1076. What's the last item I crossed off my to-do list? How did that make me feel?

1077. Is there a job I think everyone should perform in their life?

1078. Have I ever joined a club? Which was it? If not, do I want to join one?

1079. What makes a just world?

1080. Is there a keepsake in my possession? What does it mean?

1081. What's the key to someone being a good driver?

1082. When I was a kid did, I ever think adults were weird? Why?

1083. Would I ever kill an animal if I needed to hunt for food?

1084. Are people who are nice always kind?

1085. What is my favorite thing to do in a kitchen?

1086. What do I do when I know someone well?

1087. Do I believe that knowledge is power?

1088. What would I build on a newly purchased piece of land? Why?

1089. Can you speak the same language as someone and mean different things? Have I ever experienced that?

1090. What's the largest number of anything someone has offered me?

1091. The last time I lied, why did I?

1092. When have I ever thought, "Too little, too late"?

1093. What do I always leave for later?

1094. How have people described my laugh? How did that make me feel?

1095. Do I believe the law is always right?

1096. What was my last interaction with a lawyer? What was going on?

1097. When was the last time I needed a lawyer?

1098. When I lay in the grass, what is usually happening?

1099. Do I always lead?

1100. What makes someone a natural-born leader?

1101. How do I learn? Do I learn through memorization?

1102. What's my least favorite way of getting somewhere?

1103. When I leave a room, what do I always check for?

1104. When's the last time I took a left turn? Where was I going?

1105. Do I believe people that say they have a leg up on the competition?

1106. Have I ever been through legal troubles? How did I deal with it?

1107. When are the moments when less really is more?

1108. When's the last time I let someone get away with something?

1109. What was in the last handwritten letter I received?

1110. What happened the last time I saw someone really value their life? What did they do?

1111. Are there moments that need to be made lighter through humor? What are those moments?

1112. Are there two people I know that have never met but are very similar?

1113. What is the most likely thing I will say if someone is making me angry?

1114. What's my go-to line when I don't know what to say?

1115. What's the last thing I made? What was on it?

1116. Do I like making lists?

1117. What's the last song I listened to?

1118. What involves very little work?

1119. What's a big indicator of how someone lives?

1120. What's my favorite local place?

1121. How long do I have before I get really tired today?

1122. What do I always look for when I'm buying a gift?

1123. When's the last time I lost my keys? What happened?

1124. What do I think everyone should do when they suffer a loss?

1125. Is love enough?

1126. What's the lowest thing I've seen someone do?

1127. What's a machine that should exist?

1128. Who was the last person on the cover of a magazine I read? What do I think of them?

1129. What qualities should a main character in a movie always have?

1130. How do I maintain my relationships?

1131. What's a major renovation my life has gone through? Did I immediately appreciate it?

1132. What do I spend the majority of my day doing?

1133. How would someone go about making me do something I don't want to do?

1134. Who is the most important man in my life?

1135. How do I manage information overload?

1136. When was the last time I wanted to speak to a manager of an establishment?

1137. How many times have I told someone they are a good person?

1138. What's my favorite part about going to the market?

1139. What do I consider to be a bad marriage?

1140. What is my favorite material to wear?

1141. What do I think matters most to most people?

1142. Who may be the best person I could ask for advice today?

1143. Who makes me sometimes feel like they don't need me, but I know they do?

1144. Has anyone been mean to me today? How did that make me feel?

1145. How do I measure someone's goodness?

1146. Do I consume a lot of media? Should I go on a media-intake diet?

1147. Do I know my medical history? How did I become familiar with it?

1148. Who have I met recently that has made a really good impression?

1149. What's a meeting I remember vividly? What was happening?

1150. Who is the one member of my family I would never ask for help? Why?

1151. Do I have a good memory?

1152. What is the last thing I've mentioned to someone? Why?

1153. If I could leave a message to a future generation what would it be?

1154. What is a method I've developed? Why did I come up with it?

1155. What's the last thing that woke me up in the middle of the night?

1156. What might I do if someone delivered bad news today?

1157. What was the last thing I saw that I believe is one-in-a-million?

1158. What makes a healthy mind?

1159. Have I taken a one-minute break today?

1160. What's the one thing I miss from my childhood?

1161. What is my life's mission?

1162. Who should I model my life after?

1163. What do I consider modern that other people don't?

1164. Has there been a moment that made me want to take a pause today?

1165. How do I deal with money when people are involved?

1166. Where do I want to be one month from now?

1167. What do I need more of?

1168. What do I eat every morning for breakfast?

1169. What's the most I've ever cared for someone?

1170. What makes a good mother?

1171. Has anyone tried to kiss me on the mouth? What happened?

1172. Have I moved my body today?

1173. Who would star in the movie of my life?

1174. Who is the person who does much of what I ask them to do?

1175. What does music mean to the most important person of my life?

1176. What is a holiday-must everyone should do?

1177. What was my most foolish moment in life?

1178. Do I trust myself?

1179. What would I name the voice that tells me I can't do something?

1180. What makes a great nation?

1181. What do I consider to be the most natural relationship I have?

1182. Do I enjoy being in nature?

1183. Have I ever had a near-death experience?

1184. Nearly everyone I know does this? What is it?

1185. Does a necessary evil actually exist? If so, what is it?

1186. Have I cultivated a network of like-minded professionals I could ask for help when I need to?

1187. What is the one thing I said I would never do, but life had different plans?

1188. If I were catching up with an old friend, what would I say is new in my life?

1189. When I watch the news how do I feel?

1190. Do I like reading the newspaper? What's my favorite about it? What's my least favorite about it?

1191. What's next for me today?

1192. Who was nice to me today?

1193. What do I consider to be heaven on earth?

1194. When was the last time I said no to someone?

1195. What is my figurative north star?

1196. What's not on the bucket list but should be?

1197. What was the last note I wrote to someone?

1198. Have I ever given someone a two-week notice? Why?

1199. What is the last new thing I've learned about myself?

1200. What's the number of times I've had to pick myself up after falling?

1201. Of all the things I've been through, which am I proud that I overcame?

1202. What do I always turn off after using? Do I wish I could do the same to someone?

1203. What's the best thing someone has offered me?

1204. When do my best ideas often come to me?

1205. Who would be the first person to call me if I struck oil?

1206. What is the last thing I said "okay" to?

1207. When something gets old, do I make sure to keep it until it breaks down and I can't use it, or do I replace it right away? Why?

1208. What do I like to do on my birthday? Why?

1209. What was the last thing that happened only once and then never again?

1210. What's #1 on today's list of things that need to happen?

1211. Who is the only person who can always make me laugh?

1212. Do I sleep with the window open? Why or why not?

1213. Have I ever had an operation?

1214. What do I consider to be a good opportunity?

1215. What is an option I always have?

1216. What is the order of my priorities?

1217. Do I value organization or chaos?

1218. Who is the other person I go to for help all the time?

1219. Right now, at this moment, do I care what others think of me?

1220. Is there anything in my life that can be referred to as "ours"?

1221. Have I ever seen someone throw things out of a window?
What was happening?

1222. When I look outside at this moment, what do I see? What's the
first thing I noticed?

1223. Over the course of the last five years, what have I learned?

1224. What can I call my own?

1225. Do I consider myself the owner of my feelings?

1226. What's the last page I've read in a book that changed my life?

1227. Can I withstand physical pain?

1228. Can I withstand emotional pain?

1229. What's the most important piece of paper I own?

1230. The last time I saw a good parent, what were they doing?

1231. What part of my day is usually my favorite?

1232. How can I be a better participant in my community?

1233. Is there a particular brand I am loyal to?

1234. What do I consider to be a good business partner?

1235. What's the most boring party I've ever been to?

1236. Who have I given a pass to recently?

1237. When does the past affect the present?

1238. Have I been a patient person today?

1239. Do I have a pattern?

1240. What's the last thing I paid for?

1241. Where can I go right now to get some peace?

1242. Do I believe people are considerate?

1243. Have I ever experienced performance anxiety? What was happening?

1244. Is there a person who scares me?

1245. What do I consider to be too personal?

1246. Who's the first person that pops on my phone? Do I talk to them often?

1247. What's the last physical activity I partook in?

1248. Did I get picked last in gym class? What did that feel like?

1249. Who do I picture in my mind when I think about "failure"?

1250. What is the place I can go to no matter what, and I will always be relaxed?

1251. What's the last plan I made? Did I execute it?

1252. Do I like plants?

1253. Do I become a different person when I play a game?

1254. Who is my favorite sports athlete?

1255. What's the last point someone has made that I agreed with?

1256. What's my last encounter with the police?

1257. What's one of my personal policies?

1258. Have I ever performed poorly at something? What was it?

1259. Have I ever been popular?

1260. What do I believe the general population needs to know?

1261. How do I sleep? On my back, stomach, or side?

1262. Am I inherently a positive person?

1263. What do I always consider to be possible?

1264. Do I believe power corrupts?

1265. Do I practice what I preach?

1266. How do I prepare myself for challenges?

1267. What's the last present someone got me?

1268. What would I do if I were president?

1269. What caused me to put pressure on myself recently?

1270. What's something pretty I've seen recently?

1271. How do I prevent myself from getting bitter about the world?

1272. What's the best price I've ever negotiated?

1273. Have I ever been to a private beach?

1274. What is probably the best thing that happens to most people?

1275. What kind of problem solver am I?

1276. Is there a process I've tried to skip but realized I couldn't?

1277. What's the one product I wish I didn't have to buy?

1278. What teacher or professor has had a great impact in my life?

1279. Have I ever programmed myself to think a certain way?

1280. Have I ever made myself commit to a project I wasn't passionate about?

1281. Would I ever like to own property?

1282. Who protects me?

1283. Do I need to prove myself to someone?

1284. Who do I provide for?

1285. What's public in my life?

1286. Who has pull over my life?

1287. What purpose does introspection serve in my life?

1288. When push comes to shove, who do I reluctantly go to?

1289. Who was the last person to put me in my place?

1290. Do I believe in quality over quantity?

1291. What is the one question I always ask?

1292. How quickly can I get over someone?

1293. Do I believe it is about the race or the pace?

1294. Do I enjoy listening to the radio? Why?

1295. When I raise concerns? Do I feel heard?

1296. What is my range of expertise when it comes to dealing with people?

1297. What is the rate of growth I've had in my life?

1298. Would I rather show someone or tell someone that they are important to me?

1299. How do I show them?

1300. When I reach a goal, do I tend to be celebratory or be low key about it?

1301. What do I like to read? Books or articles?

1302. When did I know I was ready to be an adult?

1303. What makes a real person?

1304. Who makes a fake person?

1305. What are my views on reality TV?

1306. When did I realize I wanted to learn more about myself?

1307. Do I believe science is important? How?

1308. What was the reason for my last bout of laughter?

1309. Do I receive compliments well?

1310. What is the most recent event that may have an impact on my life forever?

1311. What do I recognize in others that I see in myself?

1312. What's the last thing I recorded on my phone? Why?

1313. When I see the color red, what do I think about?

1314. How do I reduce the amount of time I spend on others and not myself?

1315. When I reflect on my life, how do I feel?

1316. How do I relate to people?

1317. Who do I relate to the most?

1318. What's the most important thing in a relationship?

1319. Am I a religious person?

1320. How do I remain calm during adverse moments?

1321. What I remember most from my teenage years?

1322. When was the last time I removed items that I do not need from my immediate space?

1323. Did I like writing book reports in school? What did I like or dislike about them?

1324. Who best represents me?

1325. What do I believe should be a requirement for people who are considering parenthood?

1326. Do I enjoy research? Why?

1327. What is a resource I always use and encourage people to use it more often?

1328. How do I respond to people who think I can't do something?

1329. Is it my responsibility to tell someone they are wrong?

1330. Did I rest today?

1331. What is a result of my commitment to getting to know myself?

1332. What is the last item I returned? Why did I return it?

1333. What do I believe people should reveal about themselves right away?

1334. What is my definition of rich?

1335. What do I believe is an inalienable right?

1336. When did I rise to meet a task?

1337. Have I ever risked my life?

1338. What do I love about being on the road?

1339. Do I know how to skip a rock on water?

1340. Who is my role model?

1341. What is my favorite room in a house?

1342. What was a rule I hated when I was kid?

1343. When I run, what do I like listening to?

1344. When have I felt safe?

1345. Do I save money the way I should?

1346. Have I ever told myself I love myself out loud? Should I do it more often?

1347. What is the biggest scene I've caused? If not, have I ever wanted to?

1348. What do I like about school?

1349. Do I believe in science vs. nurture?

1350. Who would I hire to score the soundtrack to my life?

1351. Have I ever been seasick?

1352. Have I ever come in second in a competition? What did it feel like?

1353. Is there a section of a store I always go to?

1354. What do I consider security?

1355. Who do I see when I close my eyes and think about the happiest I was when I was a kid?

1356. What do I always seek, no matter where I am?

1357. Who do I know always seems calm but is really freaking out?

1358. Is there anything I would like to sell?

1359. When's the last time I sent something through the mail? Was it important?

1360. When I'm a senior citizen, how do I want to be?

1361. Do I have sense for my natural abilities?

1362. What's a series of events that would change history?

1363. Am I too serious about things?

1364. If I think about the one thing that frustrates me, and I ask myself, "Does this serve me?" How do I feel?

1365. Do I put a lot of importance into good service at restaurant?

1366. What time is my alarm always set to?

1367. What do I believe are the seven habits of people who are not successful?

1368. How do I view sex?

1369. Has someone come to my life to shake things up?

1370. Do I believe the world should be more forgiving?

1371. What have I seen someone shoulder that they shouldn't have?

1372. What shows me that someone really cares?

1373. What makes a good sister?

1374. How do I share the best parts of me with people?

1375. Who is someone I would hire to speak at every high school graduation?

1376. How can I detect a lie? Have I ever detected one?

1377. Who can I say is the best person in the entire world?

1378. Have I ever dreamt about being in a photo shoot?

1379. Do people consider me to be short or tall? Is that important to me?

1380. When was the last I had one shot at something?

1381. Can I describe what I see when I look to my right?

1382. What is a sign I always look for when I'm unsure about something?

1383. What do I consider to be a significant amount of money?

1384. Who is most similar to me?

1385. Do I make things simple or complicated?

1386. When was the last time I sang in the shower?

1387. Is there a dangerous situation I've been able to talk myself out of?

1388. What was happening in my life when I was six years old?

1389. What's a skill I have that surprises most people?

1390. Do I take care of my skin? How do I do that?

1391. When I was a small child, what did I think about often?

1392. Who has my favorite smile in the whole world?

1393. Do I consider myself a social person? Why?

1394. What's the one rule in society I wish others didn't need to abide by?

1395. What was my last encounter with a soldier?

1396. What makes a good son?

1397. What is a song I wish I had written?

1398. What needs to happen very soon?

1399. How do I sort through the things in my life that matter most?

1400. What is my favorite sound in the entire world?

1401. What is the source of all my joy?

1402. When was the last time that things went south really fast?

1403. What is my favorite southern custom?

1404. How do I take care and honor the physical space I take up?

1405. When I speak, am I careful with my words?

1406. When people tell me I'm special, do I believe them?

1407. If I search "inspirational speech" on an internet search engine, what comes up? Am I tempted to listen?

1408. Are sports important? Why or why not?

1409. What's a personal standard I have that most people would think is silly?

1410. If I had a star named after me, who would most likely be the person to do that for me?

1411. Do I find it difficult to start things?

1412. What is the state of my mind right now? Calm or overloaded?

1413. What would be my personal mission statement if I had to write it down?

1414. How do I stay healthy?

1415. What excites me about the world right now?

1416. What is the first step to solving every problem?

1417. When I stay still, what is the first thing that comes to mind?

1418. If I were a stock, would I be up or down right now?

1419. Have I ever been able to stop myself from going to a dark place? How did I do it?

1420. What is my favorite store to go to?

1421. What's my story? Can I sum it up in five words?

1422. Have I created a strategy for my life?

1423. What street did I grow up on? Can I describe it?

1424. What is the measure of true strength?

1425. Is there a way to structure my life so that I can always be in control?

1426. What was my favorite experience as a student?

1427. When it came to studying in school, did I like it? Or could I have been better at it?

1428. Do I have a lot of stuff?

1429. Do I have a personal style? How would I describe it?

1430. What was the subject of the last email I sent? Could it have been better?

1431. When I close my eyes and think about success, who do I see?

1432. What do I notice about successful people?

1433. What suddenly became my favorite thing ever?

1434. Have I suffered needlessly? Why?

1435. What's the last suggestion someone made to me? How did I receive it?

1436. What's underneath my surface at this very moment?

1437. If I could table one thing in my life until further notice, what would it be?

1438. Who is a great giver and taker in my life?

1439. Do I like to talk?

1440. If I could teach a class to the entire world, what would it be?

1441. Who are the people I would want on my team?

1442. Do I believe technology will solve the world's problems?

1443. What television show can I always watch regardless of how I'm feeling?

1444. If I could write my own ten commandments what would those be?

1445. What's a tendency of mine that I dislike but has always served me well?

1446. Have I ever tested someone without them knowing, and they failed? What was that like?

1447. Who is more themselves than anyone I know?

1448. Did you ever have a theory that was proven right? What was it?

1449. The last time I thought someone was nice, what happened?

1450. What is the current biggest threat to my life?

1451. What are the top three things I think about on a daily basis?

1452. Have I worked through something vs. working around it?

1453. What is the most constant thing throughout my life?

1454. When's the last time I threw a party? Did I enjoy myself?

1455. Do I believe time is our biggest friend or enemy?

1456. What kind of day did I want? Did it happen? How?

1457. Is there a couple that is still together that surprises me? Why?

1458. How can I make tonight special?

1459. What is at the top of my list of books I need to read?

1460. Can I be tougher? How?

1461. What am I working toward?

1462. What is the most beautiful town I've ever visited?

1463. If I could trade two things in my life who would I trade them with?

1464. Do I consider myself traditional? Why or why not?

1465. What is the most traditional thing I've ever done?

1466. What is the most untraditional thing I've ever done?

1467. What's one treat I could give myself today?

1468. Who treats me well all the time?

1469. Do I sense trouble before it comes my way? When have I sensed it?

1470. What did I think was true but found out otherwise?

1471. Do I believe there are different versions of the truth?
When have I see that happen?

1472. What is the one thing I always try?

1473. Have I ever given someone my turn when I was waiting in line?
Why did I do that?

1474. Do I think that TV shown me the world as it is or as I want it to be?

1475. Who is my #2?

1476. What is my type of romantic partner?

1477. What's something I wish I understood earlier than I did?

1478. How do I value my friendships?

1479. Have I ever been a victim of something?

1480. How do I view the world?

1481. Is there ever a time I would condone violence?

1482. Who was the last person I visited at a hospital?

1483. When was the last time I lost my voice? Was it inconvenient?

1484. When was the last time I went for a long walk?

1485. What's the last thing I put up on a wall? Why?

1486. What are my views on war?

1487. What is at the top of my watch list?

1488. Do I like drinking water?

1489. If I were to own a weapon what kind weapon would it be?

1490. What does what I wear say about me?

1491. What kind of day have I had?

1492. What kind of week have I had?

1493. What kind of month have I had?

1494. Do I struggle with my weight? Why or why not?

1495. If I could make an announcement to the whole world, what would it be?

1496. What should be widely known but isn't?

1497. What do I believe makes a good wife?

1498. What would I leave in my will?

1499. What's the biggest win in my life?

1500. When's the last time I was outside and felt the wind?

1501. What would my three wishes if there was a lamp and genie?

1502. Who is the most powerful woman I know?

1503. Do I have a sense of wonder toward the world?

1504. What is my favorite word?

1505. What is my least favorite word?

1506. What excites me most about work right now?

1507. What do I worry about most in the world?

1508. What would be an extravagance I would have in my yard if I could?

1509. What has been the worst year of my life?

1510. If I had a year of "yes" what would be the first thing I do?

1511. What are my views on youth?

1512. What's the worst car crash I've ever seen? What did I think about when I saw it?

1513. If I could invent a magic cream what would it be for?

1514. Do I consider myself a creative person?

1515. What is the scariest creature I have ever encountered?

1516. Who have I given credit to recently?

1517. What was the last crisis someone asked me to solve?

1518. What are my criteria for a fun time?

1519. Has there been a constructive critique that actually changed my life?

1520. If I could grow a crop of one item, what would it be?

1521. Who is the last person I saw cry in front of me? What was I thinking?

1522. What always sparks my curiosity?

1523. What is a daily practice I want to start? What is stopping me?

1524. Have I ever unknowingly damaged a friendship?

1525. When was the last time I played truth or dare? Which do I always pick?

1526. What makes a good daughter?

1527. Has someone ever declared their love to me?

1528. What is the last invitation I declined?

1529. What is the last invitation I accepted?

1530. How can I decrease the amount of time I spend on my screen?

1531. What is the one thing that someone has said to me that has deeply changed me?

1532. Have I ever had to defend myself in any way? Why?

1533. Was I successful in defending myself?

1534. Do I believe that one thing could define a person?

1535. What's the strangest conversation I've heard in public?

1536. What's the strangest conversation I've ever heard because I was eavesdropping?

1537. What was the last major delay I've experienced? How did that make me feel?

1538. Have I ever made a demand that wasn't met? Why did I make it?

1539. What is the best way to demonstrate to someone that I am the best person to perform a task?

1540. Have I ever denied something that I knew to be true? Why?

1541. When people ask for my help, what do they usually ask help for?

1542. Has my happiness ever depended on someone?

1543. How would I describe anger to a child?

1544. How would I describe love to a child?

1545. How would I describe war to a child?

1546. How would I describe the concept of crime to a child?

1547. Do I believe people deserve punishment? Why or why not?

1548. How do I feel about designer clothing?

1549. What do I believe is the main thing that drives desire?

1550. What do I always have on my desk? Why is this important?

1551. Have I ever done something out of desperation? Why?

1552. Do I hold a conviction that is truly inconsequential, but I still hold on to it anyway?

1553. Have I ever saved the life of someone? If not, what should I tell people about it if it happened?

1554. If I could destroy one thing, what would it be?

1555. Do I consider myself to be a detail-oriented person?

1556. If money and time were not an object, what hobby would I take on?

1557. What do people know me for?

1558. If I had to give a TED talk on the fly, what topic would I be able to talk about without preparing?

1559. If I became a sculptor, what would I sculpt?

1560. Throughout my life, what has been the one thing I had to unlearn?

1561. Who would I devote more time if I could?

1562. If I never had to sleep, what would I do with all that extra time?

1563. What's the worst diet I've ever been on? Why was it so bad?

1564. How do I deal with a difference of opinion?

1565. Have I ever given thought to how I would deal with a disability?

1566. What's the one stereotype I live up to? Am I ashamed of that?

1567. Do I have an irrational fear?

1568. Have I ever taken something for granted?

1569. Have I ever disappeared on someone?

1570. What's the one natural disaster I fear?

1571. Was I ever disciplined as a child? How?

1572. If I wrote a memoir and I separated it into three parts, what would be the name of those parts?

1573. What is the most important thing I've discovered about someone else?

1574. Have I ever been discriminated against? How would/did I deal with it?

1575. If I was dying, what would I want my last words to be?

1576. If another me existed in another dimension, what would they be like? What would they be doing?

1577. Is there a disorder I wish never existed?

1578. Am I someone who enjoys public displays of affection?

1579. Do I believe long distance relationships are the wrong distance?

1580. Is there a distant relative I wish I were closer to? What's stopping me from reaching out?

1581. If I could design my own car, what would the most prominent features be?

1582. Is there something I am insecure about? Why?

1583. If I were able to grant three people one wish, who would those people be?

1584. What's the farthest I've ever been away from my home?

1585. What film would I like to live in?

1586. Are there any songs I know by heart?

1587. What crazy pet have I always wanted to have?

1588. What do I believe divides human kind?

1589. Do I believe in divorce?

1590. Is there a trend I hope returns?

1591. Have I ever done something that's risky in the moment but ended up well enough?

1592. If I were a doctor would I have a good bedside manner?

1593. What is the most important document I own?

1594. Am I cat person?

1595. Do I enjoy domestic life?

1596. What is my most dominant trait?

1597. What has left me in pieces?

1598. When was the last time I slammed the door? Why?

1599. Have I ever doubled down in my life? What came of it?

1600. Has there been someone I've doubted but proved me wrong?

1601. What kind of downtown life would I lead if I could?

1602. The last time I saw someone get a dozen roses, what did I think?

1603. Is it hard for me to write a first draft of something? Why do I think that is?

1604. Have I ever dragged someone somewhere? How did that make me feel?

1605. Do I enjoy personal drama?

1606. Who is the most dramatic person I know?

1607. Can I describe the most beautiful dress I've ever seen?

1608. Do I like to drink?

1609. What's the last thing I had to air dry? Why?

1610. Do I have anything due soon?

1611. What is the best thing I've ever seen?

1612. When was the last time I wiped dust off something?

1613. What is the one civic duty I believe in wholeheartedly?

1614. What is the one civic duty we should do away with?

1615. When was the last time I was eager to see someone?

1616. Has anyone ever pulled my ear? Why?

1617. Do I like getting up early?

1618. What is the one thing I believe everyone should earn?

1619. Do my earnings define who I am as a person?

1620. What is the one thing that would save planet earth?

1621. What eases me?

1622. How easily do I adapt?

1623. What's the last thing I ate?

1624. Have I ever educated myself on something? What was the result of it?

1625. Do I know how to hard boil an egg? Who taught me?

1626. Who is an elderly person I admire?

1627. Have I ever been electrically shocked? Have I seen that happen to someone?

1628. Who do I consider to be the elite in my industry?

1629. Am I someone who enjoys writing emails?

1630. Who was the last person I embraced?

1631. What has been the scariest thing I've seen emerge from water?

1632. What was the last emergency I experienced?

1633. How would I explain emotion to a young child?

1634. Am an emotional person? Does it bother me?

1635. When was the last time I ever stood in an empty apartment or house? What was going on?

1636. Do I know someone who is an enabler?

1637. What was the last encounter I had with someone that was impactful?

1638. Do I encourage someone on a daily basis? Why?

1639. Do I believe in happy endings?

1640. Can an enemy motivate someone? How?

1641. How do I channel my unused energy?

1642. How do I engage with people who are fundamentally different than me?

1643. What powers up my emotional engine?

1644. How can I be the best engineer of my life?

1645. What is my favorite word not in my native language?

1646. Would I like anything about enhanced?

1647. What did I enjoy most last week?

1648. Who has the most enormous heart?

1649. Is there such a thing as enough affection?

1650. The last time I entered a room, who noticed me?

1651. How do I usually entertain myself?

1652. Have I ever eaten an entire pizza in one sitting?

1653. What is my all-time favorite episode of a TV show?

1654. What makes all people equal?

1655. Have I ever caught an error of mine before it was seen by the world? How did that make me feel?

1656. Where would I go if I escaped my life?

1657. Do I consider myself a perfectionist? Am I proud of that?

1658. Have I ever written an essay I am still very proud of?

1659. What are my views on ethics?

1660. Is there a European country I would visit tomorrow? Why?

1661. How do I evaluate someone?

1662. What would I consider to be the thrill of a lifetime?

1663. Have ever evened the score with someone?

1664. Have I ever exceeded expectations? How did it feel?

1665. When was the last time I made an exception?

1666. What was the last time I had someone tell me I was excellent?

1667. How would I go about expanding my horizons?

1668. Have I ever tried explaining myself and failed miserably? Why?

1669. What was my last big expense? Why?

1670. When was the last time I experimented?

1671. If I had a farm what would be the main thing it would be known for?

1672. Who do I want to go on vacation with?

1673. Am I at fault for the last argument I had with someone?

1674. When is the last time I asked someone for a favor? Do I do it often?

1675. Do I have a favorite shirt?

1676. When I feel fear, what do I do?

1677. What is one feature of mine I wish everyone noticed all the time?

1678. What would fee what I charge for any extra work I do?

1679. What feeds my soul?

1680. How do I feel at this very moment?

1681. Have I ever jumped a fence?

1682. What has been the best fiction story I've ever read?

1683. What did I do for my fifteenth birthday?

1684. If I was turning 100 years old, how would I want to celebrate that milestone?

1685. What do I want to accomplish by the time I am fifty years old?

1686. Do I consider myself a lover or a fighter?

1687. How would I fill my day today if I had it my way?

1688. Is there a film I wish I had made?

1689. What is the last thing I fixed?

1690. The last time I saw a bouquet of flowers, what was I doing?

1691. What is my favorite slang word?

1692. When was the last time I went to a football game?

1693. Do I believe in forever?

1694. When I forget something who usually reminds of it?v

1695. What is the formula to success? Is there one?

1696. If I had a fortune, what would I want done with it when I passed?

1697. How could I pay it forward?

1698. What's the last thing I looked for and found?

1699. What is the foundation of a good relationship?

1700. If I were the founder of a club, which one would it be?

1701. What condiment do I hate the most?

1702. When was the last time I had brain-freeze?

1703. What's my favorite French word?

1704. What's my favorite fresh drink of choice on a hot summer day?

1705. What is the one thing every friend should be able to do?

1706. Is there a land I consider to be forgotten?

1707. What did I do during my last vacation?

1708. Has someone ever given me money when I needed it?

1709. What's my favorite fruit?

1710. When is the last time I had a meal that left very full?

1711. What would make me feel like I had the world at my fingertips?

1712. What do I always consider to be fun no matter what mood I am in?

1713. Does everyone need to serve a function in my life?

1714. If I had unlimited funds, would life be better?

1715. What is the biggest enigma in my life?

1716. Who leans on me?

1717. Do I have self-control?

1718. When do I feel most blessed?

1719. If I were a piece of furniture what would I be? Why?

1720. What is the one thing I'm still into since I was a kid?

1721. What did I like the most about going back to school in the fall?

1722. Am I always prepared to have a good time?

1723. What animal do I want to be more like?

1724. Have I ever threatened someone and had it work?

1725. If could go anywhere in the galaxy, where would I go?

1726. What moments would a gallery of my life contain?

1727. What's been a moment where I thought I was going to come up short, but didn't?

1728. How have I closed the largest gap in knowledge I've had?

1729. What's the funniest thing I've seen stored in a garage?

1730. Is there ever such a thing as too much garlic in food?

1731. What is the funniest thing that has happened to me at a gas station?

1732. What's a genetic mutation I wish I had?

1733. Do I believe in ghosts?

1734. What's a gift I wish I had?

1735. Who is the most gifted person I know?

1736. Have I ever pressed my face unto a store window?

1737. What would I give the most important person in my life at all times if I had it?

1738. When's the last time I was glad to see someone?

1739. At a quick glance what celebrity would I be confused with?

1740. Is there a global movement I wish I had experienced?

1741. If I had to have something I love plated in gold, what would I pick?

1742. Have I ever played golf?

1743. What makes something good for me?

1744. What's the first thing I grab when I have to leave the house in a hurry?

1745. What grade was I in when I learned that humans are mammals?

1746. If I had to come up with something to graduate from, what would it be?

1747. What do I take with a grain of salt?

1748. What is the best memory I have of my grandfather?

1749. What is the best memory I have of my grandmother?

1750. Who would be the person to grant me a wish if they could?

1751. When was the last time I walked on the grass?

1752. Have I ever visited someone's grave? Who was it?

1753. What is the one thing I always buy when I grocery shop?

1754. What is the quirkiest thing I am known for?

1755. Have I ever guarded my heart?

1756. When was the last time I felt guilty about something?

1757. What is the best hairstyle I've ever had?

1758. Do I have a favorite hat?

1759. Have I ever hated someone?

1760. Has there been a newspaper headline that made me laugh? What was it?

1761. If I were the head of a company, what would the company headquarters look like?

1762. How could people value their health more?

1763. Do I enjoy being in the heat?

1764. What is my height? Has someone every commented on it?

1765. Where would I ride a helicopter to?

1766. What's the most helpful thing someone has said to me?

1767. Do I believe heroes are born not made? Why?

1768. If someone made a highlight reel of my life, what would on it?

1769. If I were an historian, what would I focus on?

1770. Is honor something that is important to me?

1771. Is there hope in the horizon?

1772. Have I ever petted a horse? What was that like?

1773. If I were hunting, what would I be thinking about?

1774. The last time I was hurt, what did I do?

1775. What makes a good husband?

1776. Have I ever had to put ice on injury? What was the injury?

1777. What are the ideal conditions for me to be my most creative?

1778. Is there something that is illegal that I feel should be illegal? What is it?

1779. Has someone ever implied I'm not good at something? How did that make me feel?

1780. What is my biggest incentive?

1781. Who do I always include in my plans?

1782. Who do I consider to be an incredible person?

1783. Have I ever been injured?

1784. What's some insight I offered someone recently that made a difference?

1785. Am I emotionally intelligent?

1786. Am I addicted something?

1787. What's the last piece of clothing I ironed?

1788. Do I like to iron?

1789. Do I have a favorite Italian dish?

1790. What is an item on my to-do list I always cross out?

1791. When's the last time I wore a jacket?

1792. What's my favorite joke?

1793. Did I ever learn to jump rope as a kid?

1794. Do I know how to double Dutch?

1795. Who deserved to get a kiss, but I didn't give it?

1796. Did I ever deserve to be kissed by someone but I didn't get that kiss?

1797. Do I like cleaning the kitchen? What do I hate or like most about it?

1798. What's a knee jerk reaction I've had recently?

1799. What's a label I hate having?

1800. What's a label I wear proudly?

1801. When was the last time I did something I knew was going to hurt me, but I did it anyway?

1802. When was the last time I did something I knew was going to be good for me?

1803. Do I like to stay up late? Why?

1804. Do I like to go to bed early? Why?

1805. Who was the last person I heard laughing? Why were they laughing?

1806. Is there an urban legend that scares me?

1807. Is there an urban legend I wish were true? Why?

1808. When have I ever made lemonade out of lemons?

1809. Do I have a driver's license? Was it hard?

1810. If I could describe my lifestyle in one word, what would it be?

1811. What do I want to see happen in my lifetime?

1812. Is there something that I've made light of that I shouldn't have?

1813. Have I ever had a limitation?

1814. What's my constant link to my family?

1815. What's my favorite piece of literature?

1816. When I was little what was my favorite stuffed animal?

1817. What is my long-term vision for my life? Do I have one?

1818. What personal maintenance do I perform on myself that always makes me feel good?

1819. Do I have a vivid memory of going to the mall when I was young? What was it?

1820. Am I good at reading maps?

1821. Do I like writing in the margins of books?

1822. Have I ever worn a mask?

1823. Am I good at math?

1824. What matters most to me today? Does it change day to day?

1825. What's the best piece of medical advice I've ever gotten?

1826. Have I ever enjoyed taking medicine?

1827. Have I ever been able to meet someone's expectations?

1828. How do I take care of my mental health?

1829. If I could create a menu what would be at the top?

1830. Do I have what it takes to join the military?

1831. Have I ever witnessed a miracle?

1832. Have I ever broken a mirror?

1833. What am I good at moderating for myself?

1834. Am I a modest person?

1835. When's the last time I saw a full moon?

1836. What do I wish my mornings were like?

1837. What is the best way to describe what my mornings are actually like?

1838. What is my own personal mountain? Have I conquered it?

1839. When's the last time I saw a mouse? Did it scare me?

1840. Have I ever pulled a muscle? How did it happen?

1841. Have I ever stood in front of a mirror naked and looked at myself?

1842. What is my favorite Greek myth?

1843. Did I know what my parents would have named had I been assigned a different gender?

1844. Have I ever lost necklace? Was it important?

1845. Am I a good negotiator?

1846. Am I good neighbor? Could I be a better neighbor?

1847. How would I describe my neighborhood?

1848. How has my neighborhood changed since I moved into it?

1849. Have I ever broken my nose? How? If not, have I almost broken it?

1850. Am I allergic to anything? If so, has it ever stopped me from doing something?

1851. Have I ever been camping?

1852. If I could make my own food pyramid, what would I place on the top and bottom?

1853. If I could talk about anything right now, what would topic would I choose?

1854. Is there an obligation I don't mind having?

1855. Has anyone made an observation about me that was spot on?

1856. Does the ocean scare me?

1857. Am I good at multi-tasking?

1858. What's my favorite room in a school?

1859. What am I very happy with at the moment?

1860. Have I ever been so disappointed in something that I wanted to cry?

1861. What's the most offensive thing I've ever heard?

1862. What's the most offensive thing I've ever said?

1863. What's the hardest thing I've ever done?

1864. What is the worst apology I've ever gotten?

1865. What is the best apology I've ever heard?

1866. When is an apology no longer helpful?

1867. Have I ever walked out of a movie theater in the middle of a movie?

1868. Have I ever seen a movie more than once at the movie theater?

1869. On a scale of one to ten, how much do I dislike going into the office?

1870. On a scale of one to ten, how much do I like working from home?

1871. Have I ever needed to be talked into something? What was it?

1872. What is the next thing I want to attempt?

1873. What is an ongoing project I have going on?

1874. Whose opinion do I care about the most?

1875. Whose opinion do I care about the least? Why?

1876. Is there a job I would never want to have?

1877. How did I go about solving a problem someone else couldn't solve?

1878. What is the most extraordinary thing about me?

1879. What is the most organic friendship I have?

1880. Is there a question I will always refuse to answer?

1881. How do I organize my drawers?

1882. Was there a time where silence scared me?

1883. What song has the power to remind me of my childhood?

1884. Is there a tragedy that I think could have been avoided?

1885. What's the most stressful problem I've ever faced?

1886. Who is the person who I see most in myself?

1887. Has something been placed in my care before? Did I do a good job?

1888. What is the most extraordinary thing I've ever witnessed?

1889. Do I think about others often?

1890. When's the last time I was overcome with emotion?

1891. Do I owe someone a favor?

1892. Who is the most empathetic person I know?

1893. When was the last time I was overthinking something?

1894. Do I have a personal definition for loyalty?

1895. Do I have personal definition for betrayal?

1896. When is the last time I used a stopwatch?

1897. If I could send someone adrift, who would it be?

1898. Have I ever sulked over something? What was it?

1899. Do I believe in synchronicity between people?

1900. When was the last time I went swimming? How did it feel?

1901. Have I ever thought I was boring? Why?

1902. What was the last time I paid for a ticket? What was it for?

1903. What's my favorite kind of sandwich? Why?

1904. Have I ever been wasteful? What made me realize it?

1905. What do I like on my toast that's unusual?

1906. Have I ever raised money for a cause I believe in?

1907. Who would I be in band? The lead singer, guitar, bass player, or drummer?

1908. Do I believe in extraterrestrial life?

1909. Have I ever seen something suspicious with relation to extraterrestrial life?

1910. What was my last beach trip like?

1911. Did I want my last beach trip to be different?

1912. What's my favorite part about going to a museum?

1913. What's my least favorite part about going to a museum?

1914. When was the last time I was nervous?

1915. Have I ever played in the snow?

1916. If I had a sabbatical for one year, where would I go?

1917. When's the last time someone treated me for a meal? Did it make me feel special?

1918. When's the last time I've treated someone for a meal? Did it make me feel special?

1919. When's the last time I could not get a song out of my head?

1920. If I could rename the country, what name would I choose?

1921. If I had to choose an injury which would I pick?

1922. What's my biggest weakness?

1923. What's my biggest strength?

1924. Have I ever wanted revenge for something?

1925. Do I remember when I got my first cellphone?

1926. Do I remember the first movie I saw in the movie theater?

1927. What was the worst present I've ever gotten?

1928. What's the worst present I've ever given?

1929. What's the longest phone call I've ever had with someone?

1930. If I could bring any fictional character to life, who would it be? Why?

1931. Do I consider myself an attractive person?

1932. Have I ever shot a gun? What was it like?

1933. What's the most expensive thing I own?

1934. Have I ever faked it until I made it? Did it work?

1935. What's the greatest thing about the country I live in?

1936. What's the greatest thing about the city or town I live in?

1937. If I could talk to an animal for a day, which animal would I choose?

1938. When I was a kid, did I ever climb a tree?

1939. Have I ever climbed a tree as an adult?

1940. Have I ever been embarrassed for someone else? Why?

1941. What do I always ask on a first date?

1942. What's my biggest vice?

1943. Have I ever encountered a snake in the wild? What was that like?

1944. Do I know how to defend myself?

1945. If I could be a very famous sports athlete what sport would I choose? Why?

1946. When is the last time I played in the rain?

1947. Am I an introvert or an extrovert?

1948. Is there a video game I could play for a long period of time?

1949. Do I have a memory of my first grade teacher? Can I describe them?

1950. Do I have a memory of my second grade teacher? Can I describe them?

1951. Do I have a memory of my third grade teacher? Can I describe them?

1952. Do I have a memory of my fourth grade teacher? Can I describe them?

1953. Do I have a memory of my fifth grade teacher? Can I describe them?

1954. Have I ever gone fruit picking?

1955. Have I ever accidentally dropped something down the stairs?

1956. When was the last time I had a fever?

1957. Do I have any pets? If not, do I want pets? If yes, can I describe my pet?

1958. What's a useless skill I possess?

1959. If I could come up with my own holiday, what would it be?

1960. If I could learn a type of dance, what would I want to learn?

1961. Have I ever suffered from imposter syndrome?

1962. How did I move past my imposter syndrome?

1963. How have I dealt with burnout?

1964. What's my most significant achievement so far?

1965. Have I ever met someone who knew me before I knew them?

1966. Have I ever been on a canoe?

1967. Who am I always curious about?

1968. What's red flag for ME?

1969. When I am old, what kind of questions will I ask from younger relatives?

1970. What was the last photo I took?

1971. Who is a famous person I think is down to earth?

1972. What's the most expensive I've ever eaten?

1973. What's the most expensive thing I've ever damaged?

1974. What's more annoying to me? The hiccups or a mosquito bite?

1975. What movie quote can be used to describe life?

1976. What's the one thing I wish young children could experience but won't be able to because of the time they were born in?

1977. What was a trend when I was child? Would I want it to come back?

1978. What was a trend when I was teenager? Would I want it to come back?

1979. Do I believe having a sense of humor can make an awful situation better?

1980. What word do I love to say out loud?

1981. Do I believe that freedom is privilege or a right?

1982. Have I covered for someone? Who was it? Why did I do it?

1983. Who is the last person I got to know?

1984. Do I have an unpopular opinion?

1985. Have I ever given myself a haircut? Was it a good one?

1986. What's the last thing I saw on the road?

1987. Is there anything that I hoard?

1988. Is there someone I feel like I know but I've never met them?

1989. What's the weirdest voicemail I've ever received?

1990. What's the weirdest text message I've ever received?

1991. What's the weirdest email I've ever received?

1992. Do I have a good luck charm?

1993. Has there been a time when I've put whatever I could find on and it ended up being a great outfit?

1994. What do I define as classy?

1995. What is the quintessential summertime food?

1996. What is the quintessential wintertime food?

1997. Do I know someone who is underappreciated? Can I help them not feel that way?

1998. What's the funniest nickname someone has given me?

1999. What's the worst nickname someone has given me?

2000. Do I like to plan more or improvise more?

2001. What's the most random thing I've ever been paid for?

2002. What song lyric is the most ridiculous?

2003. What was my favorite cereal when I was growing up?

2004. When has nature made me feel small in the best way possible?

2005. Is there something most people have experienced that I haven't just yet?

2006. Is there an accent I enjoy hearing?

2007. If I could be an age forever, what age would it be?

2008. Has a text message ever scared me?

2009. If my day was a meal, what meal would it be?

2010. What was a food I liked when I was growing up that I can't stand as an adult?

2011. If I could pick a song to play every time I walked into a room, what song would it be?

2012. Are there any traditions I want to end?

2013. What's the longest amount of time I've been asleep? Why?

2014. Is there a bathroom rule everyone should adhere to?

2015. What has been the most passive-aggressive note I've ever received?

2016. Have I ever self-sabotaged myself? When?

2017. Have I ever made friends while traveling? Who comes to mind?

2018. Is there something that I was never taught but had to experience in order to learn it?

2019. What's the dumbest argument I've ever been in?

2020. What was the last concert I went to?

2021. What was the most memorable concert I've ever been to?

2022. Do I have a favorite comedian?

2023. How could I be more unique?

2024. If I could create my own personal archive, what would be in it?

2025. Have I ever been in total despair?

2026. Have I ever met someone who tried to minimize my feelings? How did I deal with it?

2027. Have I ever copied from someone?

2028. What would be a creative way to torture me?

2029. What exists in abundance in my life?

2030. How have I maintained my dignity in awful moments?

2031. Have I ever had a great encounter with a waiter?

2032. When's the last time I went to the theater?

2033. Have I ever worn silk?

2034. When is the last time someone interrupted me? How did that make me feel?

2035. When was the last time someone threw me a surprise party?

2036. What would be my campaign slogan?

2037. What is the most practical thing I've ever done?

2038. Have I ever burned any bridges?

2039. Are my relationships all about transactions?

2040. Have I been to the eye doctor recently? Do I like those visits?

2041. Has anyone ever betrayed me?

2042. What's the last announcement I made?

2043. What do I tend to splurge on?

2044. What's my favorite frozen food?

2045. Have I ever written poetry? Did I like it?

2046. Do I have the support that I need?

2047. Am I flexible person?

2048. What's the most unfortunate thing I've seen happen to someone? How did I feel?

2049. Have I ever witnessed an example of when "bad news travels fast"?

2050. Have I ever witnessed an extreme overreaction?

2051. Who have I met that seemed strange at first, but then turned out to be totally endearing?

2052. Do I believe perception is reality?

2053. What kind of photos does my favorite photo album contain?

2054. Have I ever witnessed a scandal first hand?

2055. Do I enjoy cleaning?

2056. Have I ever been stung by a bee? What was it like?

2057. What's my favorite kind of cake?

2058. What is a trait I wish I had?

2059. When was the last time I went bike riding?

2060. How do I like to decorate?

2061. What is the most virtuous thing I've ever done?

2062. When's the last time I visited the countryside? Did it relax me?

2063. Have I ever experienced an explosion of emotions?
Can I describe a moment?

2064. If I had to protest something, what would it be?

2065. What is the one thing I've never budged on?

2066. Who is definitely in heaven?

2067. Am I natural mediator? When did I realize it?

2068. If I could choose a symbol to define me, which would I pick?

2069. Have I ever pledged to do something?

2070. How do I feel when I hear someone demand something?

2071. Has there been a condition someone has not met in my life?

2072. What makes a good citizen?

2073. If I were president, instead of pardoning turkeys what animal would I pardon?

2074. When do I become an unreasonable person?

2075. When was the last time I took a bow?

2076. Have I ever lost an important document?

2077. Have I ever been uncomfortable by someone's proximity?

2078. Do I believe the world is accommodating of handicap people?

2079. If I were a dog, what breed would I be?

2080. Have I ever asked someone for advice only so that I could do the opposite of what they say?

2081. Would people say I am always accessible?

2082. What is the one award I want to win?

2083. Who is the most narrow-minded person I know?
What makes them that way?

2084. Who is the most secure person I've ever encountered?
What makes them that way?

2085. Do I tend to skip steps?

2086. What is more important in a relationship? Communication or trust?

2087. Have I ever rehearsed for something? Why?

2088. What event in the 18th century would I want to witness firsthand?

2089. What is the main thing about city-living that I am attracted to?

2090. When was the last time someone told me to watch my tone?

2091. When was the last time I wrote a check? What was it for?

2092. Have I ever smiled at a stranger? Why?

2093. What's my favorite part about visiting somewhere and being a tourist?

2094. What's the one riddle I've never been able to solve?

2095. Do I own rainboots? Why?

2096. What about today do I appreciate?

2097. Am I marriage material?

2098. Who do I know that is marriage material but has no interest in marriage?

2099. Would I choose to live in a palace alone?
Or in a small house with my entire family?

2100. When was the first time I realized I had full autonomy over my body?

2101. Do I tend to cooperate when I am in group of people?

2102. What is a rite of passage I could do without?

2103. Is there a gene I would eliminate in the human race?

2104. Have I ever been to a memorial? What was it like?

2105. Do I need to know all the facts in advance before I go into a situation?

2106. Who do I know is deserving to have a biography written
about their life? Why?

2107. Are good manners important?

2108. If I could exchange a body part for an appliance, what would I exchange?

2109. Do I devote enough time to what I love?

2110. Have I ever visited a fortune teller?

2111. What am I always aware of?

2112. Do I know anyone who things they are funny, but they are not?

2113. What would I do if I were fifteen years younger?

2114. What is the last thing I ordered through the telephone?

2115. Have I ever hidden my tears?

2116. When was the last time I bled?

2117. When's the last time I used a hammer?

2118. If had to become a reporter tomorrow, would I be good at it?

2119. Have I ever smoked a cigarette?

2120. Have I wandered aimlessly without worrying about where I am going?

2121. What is a prejudice I hold? Have I tried to overcome it?

2122. Who do I consider royalty but aren't actual royalty?

2123. Can I describe a perfect summer day?

2124. Do I believe a picture is worth a thousand words?

2125. When was the last time I was bundled up in layers of clothing? Why?

2126. Have I ever feigned happiness?

2127. Do I prefer butter or jam on my toast?

2128. Is there something I always reserve for only myself?
Does that make me selfish?

2129. Who would have something nice to say about my personal development?

2130. What am I worried about today?

2131. When was the last time I dribbled a ball?

2132. Have I ever changed a spare tire?

2133. How do I feel about winning?

2134. Do I hold any implicit bias?

2135. If life is school, am I a good student?

2136. When was the last time I saw smoke? What was happening?

2137. If I had to amputate a body part, which would I pick? Why?

2138. Have I ever done something out of spite?

2139. Do I read enough?

2140. Do I read too much?

2141. What has been a story I liked hearing about my grandfather?

2142. What has been a story I liked hearing about my grandmother?

2143. Have I ever encountered something fraudulent?

2144. How do I cope with stress?

2145. When was the last time I tidied up my surroundings? Why did I do it?

2146. Have I ever felt trapped?

2147. Have I ever entrapped myself?

2148. What is my favorite part of a new relationship?

2149. What is the best part of being in a long-time relationship?

2150. What is my favorite part of a new friendship?

2151. What is the best part of being in a long-time friendship?

2152. When I was a kid, did I ever get an allowance?

2153. What is my ideology?

2154. Have I ever sacrificed something?

2155. Is there a problem I need to solve? What am I able to do about it at this moment?

2156. What's the last package in my possession with a ribbon on it?

2157. What's worst? Noise or air pollution?

2158. Have I ever thought about something innovating?

2159. Have I ever been displaced? What was it like?

2160. Who is the purest person I know?

2161. What do I think minors should be able to do?

2162. Have I ever gotten a promotion? What did it feel like?

2163. When's the last time I held a lighter? What were the circumstances?

2164. What is the highest I've paid for the price of admission?

2165. When did I last have a meal I enjoyed?

2166. Have I ever plucked my eyebrows?

2167. Have I ever had to explain something that took a lot out of me to explain? Why?

2168. Is my definition of winning different than most?

2169. Who is the smoothest person I know?

2170. What is the one thing I would ban today?

2171. Have I ever been frowning and didn't know it until someone told me?

2172. What is a Jeopardy category I would excel in?

2173. Is there a perfect voter?

2174. Is there something I need to forbid myself from doing today?

2175. Have I ever called on someone to fix something I knew I could fix myself? Why?

2176. Do I have a mutual friend with someone I admire?

2177. How do I define strength?

2178. Am I a dramatic person?

2179. Have I ever worn high heels?

2180. Does the perfect prison exist?

2181. If I was a reigning monarch, what kind of monarch would I be?

2182. If I was a dictator, what kind of things would I do?

2183. When was the last time I ever took a nap?

2184. Do I like taking naps?

2185. What was on the last sheet of paper I held?

2186. What's the main thing that would be different in my life if I lived somewhere else?

2187. What's my favorite thing about a computer?

2188. What's my least favorite thing about a computer?

2189. Do I have a vein that protrudes when I get upset?

2190. Do I know someone who has a vein that protrudes when they are upset?

2191. Is there a date I always commemorate that is not my birthday or a major holiday?

2192. When's the last time my face was flushed?

2193. Have I ever quit something? Why?

2194. Have I ever seen someone quit something? How did I feel seeing it happen?

2195. What tethers me to the world?

2196. Do I have a personal ritual no one would understand?

2197. What's the weirdest ritual I've ever seen in person?

2198. Have I ever been in mourning for a long period of time?

2199. What makes a good diplomat?

2200. Would I be a good diplomat?

2201. When was the last time I paid a toll? What was happening?

2202. Have I ever adopted rhetoric I didn't really believe? Why?

2203. What tends to stimulates me?

2204. If I had a cellar, what would I keep in it?

2205. Does my life have structure?

2206. When's the last time I knocked on a door? Where was I trying to get into?

2207. What is central to being a good person?

2208. Do I believe misery loves company? Have I ever seen it first hand?

2209. When was the last time I saw a needle? What was going on?

2210. Do I always have a reason for the things that I do?

2211. The last time I yelled at someone, what was frustrating me?

2212. The last time I was consoling someone, was I thinking about how they've consoled me in the past?

2213. Have I ever spread someone's ashes?

2214. When is the last time I was hit by a wave at the beach?

2215. Have I ever been in a real-life maze?

2216. When was the last time I was reluctant to do something?

2217. Have I ever planted a tree?

2218. If I could plant a tree, where would I plant one?

2219. Would I look good bald?

2220. How do I adjust my attitude?

2221. What have I considered impossible but saw happen much later?

2222. When's the last time I heard a dog bark? What was happening?

2223. Did I ever want a pony as a kid?

2224. What did I love most about the toy store when I was growing up?

2225. What is the one thing I've neglected recently?

2226. What's on my bookshelf right now?

2227. How do people best express their emotions?

2228. How long has it been since I've told someone I love them?

2229. What are my views on grief?

2230. Do I have a tendency of ignoring people?

2231. Is there a shortage of something in my life? What is it?

2232. Am I part of a clique?

2233. Have I ever badmouthed someone?

2234. Have I ever reacted harshly to something but was aware that it was a warranted reaction?

2235. If I could be the heir of an empire, which would I pick?

2236. Was I good student in elementary school?

2237. What was the first school dance I went to? What is my memory if it?

2238. Have I ever talked someone through why they have a guilty conscience?

2239. Have I ever killed a plant?

2240. Have I ever been in the pitch-black dark? Was it scary?

2241. Have I ever gone swimming in the dark?

2242. Am I good house guest?

2243. What makes a good house guest?

2244. Is being picky about food a major character flaw? Why?

2245. When's the last time I saw someone wearing an ankle bracelet?

2246. What is my favorite herb to use when cooking?

2247. Who in my life drives a hard bargain?

2248. Is there someone I have contempt for?

2249. If I wanted to smile at this moment, who do I think about?

2250. Is there a limit to how much fun a person should be having?

2251. What's the one thing I've done in public that I wish I could take back?

2252. When is the last time I stained something?

2253. Can a person be too sensitive?

2254. Is there someone I know who is too sensitive?

2255. Who do I always learn from?

2256. Have I ever volunteered to a social cause?

2257. What has driven me to ecstasy?

2258. Do I recycle?

2259. If I could eliminate a color, which would it be?

2260. Who is the most tactful person I know?

2261. Is tact something I admire in a person?

2262. Am I usually in the majority or minority?

2263. Who was the last person I touched? Why?

2264. Is there a major retailer I frequent? Why?

2265. Have I ever forgotten to flush the toilet? What was going on?

2266. Have I ever studied philosophy? If not, do I want to?

2267. Have I done something recently and had to be discreet about it?

2268. What's the last white lie I told?

2269. What's the last thing I threw into the garbage bin?

2270. What has intensified the older I've gotten?

2271. What's the best response to an insult I've ever heard?

2272. What's the difference between a fact and an opinion?

2273. Have I ever been in denial over something? When did I realize it?

2274. When was the last time I used a bucket? Why?

2275. Have I ever gotten a foot rub? What was the best/worst part of it?

2276. When's the last time I "hit the pavement"?

2277. Have I ever been to therapy?

2278. Do I know someone who should be going to therapy?

2279. Have I ever told someone they should go to therapy? How did they respond?

2280. When was the last time "the calm before the storm" applied?

2281. What's the hottest temperature I've ever experienced?

2282. Have I ever been to an emergency room? What was the experience like?

2283. Have I ever disagreed with my doctor?

2284. Have I ever gone for a medical second opinion?

2285. What's the easiest thing anyone could do that has the biggest impact?

2286. Do I like cheese?

2287. Have I ever been called stubborn? What was the reason?

2288. Is there anyone in the world I consider to have accomplished world domination?

2289. Have been opposed to someone getting married? Why?

2290. When is the last time I had to reference prior correspondence I had with someone? Why?

2291. When's the last time I've closed a curtain?

2292. Have I ever fed a baby?

2293. Have I ever changed a diaper?

2294. Have I ever accidentally cursed in front of a child? Did I feel bad?

2295. What is the one thing people who communicate clearly have in common?

2296. What do I despise the most at this very moment?

2297. What is the last song I had on repeat?

2298. Have I ever been close with a next door neighbor? What are the perks?

2299. What am I average in?

2300. Have I ever broken a bone in my body? What happened?

2301. Have I ridden in the back of a pick-up truck?

2302. Have I ever played in a pile of leaves?

2303. What's the grossest thing I ever did as a kid?

2304. When's the last time I wore a helmet?

2305. Have I ever seen a deer in person?

2306. When is the last time I went on a hike?

2307. When is the last time I took a dip in a pool?

2308. When is the last time I took a long walk on the beach?

2309. Have I ever just laid in the grass?

2310. When is the last time I went to an outdoor concert? Did I enjoy it?

2311. What is the most graphic thing I've ever read?

2312. What frightens most people, but not me?

2313. What is the best sensation in the world?

2314. What kind of music do I play in the background to relax me?

2315. Is there a wild animal that I would choose to protect me at all times?

2316. Who is the last person I bothered?

2317. Is profit important to me?

2318. Have I ever acted like a chauvinist?

2319. Has there been anyone I know who has acted like chauvinist?

2320. What's the last thing I took offense to?

2321. What is the one scent that I never tire of?

2322. When is the last time I was at an orientation?

2323. What is the main characteristic of all great leaders?

2324. Have I ended a relationship only to jump into another that was a continuation of the previous one?

2325. When has my intuition been an asset?

2326. Was I hungry the last time I opened my refrigerator?

2327. Who is the tallest person I know?

2328. Who is the shortest person I know?

2329. Do I have credibility?

2330. What's the best costume I've ever seen?

2331. Have I ever run into someone at an airport?

2332. Am I at the top of someone's priority list?

2333. Has anyone ever said something inappropriate to me?

2334. How can I expand my horizons?

2335. What was the last plan I made?

2336. Have I had a recurring dream recently?

2337. What is the last book I've read that challenged me?

2338. How can I turn an insecurity into a window for opportunity?

2339. Am I ensuring I have a good day today? How?

2340. How many continents have I visited?

2341. Am I part of a hierarchy? Do I want to be higher? Lower?

2342. Have I ever been part of an intervention?

2343. Am I reliable?

2344. What is my idea of relaxation but isn't to most people?

2345. What are my favorite electronics?

2346. When's the last time I was preoccupied?

2347. When did I deviate from a plan but ended up getting the same results?

2348. Am I good with machinery?

2349. Have I ever had an operation?

2350. What would be on the dedication page of my book?

2351. What is beautiful solely because of its simplicity?

2352. What questions would I make sure is in an application to be close friend of mine?

2353. What is the common thread of all great civilizations?

2354. What is the common thread of all civilizations that ended?

2355. If I could create a coalition, what would I name it?

2356. What was the last presentation I gave?

2357. Who was the last person I took into consideration while making a decision?

2358. What was the best meal I had outdoors? What was so great about it?

2359. What is the worst rumor I've ever heard?

2360. What is the funniest rumor I've ever heard?

2361. What rumor do I know is true?

2362. What's the longest book I've ever tried to read? Did I finish it?

2363. What makes me cry just thinking about it?

2364. Do I know someone who wears a prosthesis? Do I know the backstory?

2365. When is the last time I was absorbed into a project? What was it?

2366. What is the last thing I recorded on my phone?

2367. Have I ever resold something? Why did I resell it?

2368. If I were famous, would I always look for the spotlight?

2369. What signifies to me that someone knows who they are?

2370. What was the last meal I prepared that didn't come out the way I wanted it to?

2371. Do I prefer beef or chicken?

2372. What grade was I in when I made the best memories?

2373. Have I ever been graded on a curve?

2374. Do I know a dysfunctional family?

2375. What is the difference between a functional and dysfunctional family?

2376. Who would I trust to have my power of attorney?

2377. What's the last book that made me laugh?

2378. What's the last book that made me cry?

2379. Have I ever made a declaration I had to take back?

2380. Is there a photograph in my eyesight? What would the best caption for it?

2381. What do I take way to seriously?

2382. When was the last time I threw a ball?

2383. Does thunder scare me?

2384. Does lightening scare me?

2385. When was the last time a zipper broke?

2386. Am I an overachiever?

2387. Is there a note someone wrote to me that I kept?

2388. What do I consider to be the most lamentable experience?

2389. When was the last time I slipped and fell?

2390. Who is the clumsiest person I know?

2391. Who makes me a better person?

2392. What's the one rule that can always be bent?

2393. Do I remember the last time my parents punished me?

2394. What do I always carry with me? Why?

2395. If I could be a tour guide, where would I give tours?

2396. Have I ever seen two people be envious of one another?

2397. What's the one thing I would erase from my school record?

2398. When's the last time I blew up a balloon?

2399. When was the last time someone gave me a hug and thanked me? How did that make me feel?

2400. What is my favorite thing about a birthday party?

2401. What is the one thing every birthday party needs?

2402. When was the last time I played pin the tail on the donkey?

2403. If I was driving a convertible and had the top down, what song would I play really loudly?

2404. Is there a music video I wished I lived in?

2405. Have I ever had a sloppy kiss? Who was it with?

2406. Do I carry cash with me? Why?

2407. What is the quickest I've ever been disinterested in someone? Why?

2408. Do I become stressed when I get too busy?

2409. What is the most foolish thing I've heard someone say in public?

2410. Who is my rock?

2411. When was the last time I got dizzy? Why?

2412. When was the last time I felt like an outsider?

2413. When was the last time I felt like a gatekeeper?

2414. What do I consider to be tranquil environment?

2415. Have I ever been capricious?

2416. When was the last time I had a cold?

2417. Do I know someone who speaks in a lyrical way?

2418. Who of the people that I know has the most spotless home?

2419. Who has the most deadpan sense of humor of everything I know?

2420. Who can I always talk to and have a great conversation with?

2421. How do I resolve conflict?

2422. What's the last thing I had to use glue for?

2423. Have I ever tried yoga?

2424. What is the most well-made item I own?

2425. Have I ever been the villain in someone else's story?

2426. Have I ever solved a misunderstanding?

2427. Have I ever been in an earthquake? What did it feel like?

2428. Who is the most attractive person I know?

2429. Is there a version of myself from a long time ago I wish I could bring back? Why?

2430. Who are the people I consider to be in my inner circle? Can I describe them?

2431. If I could make up a whole new life? Where would I go? What would I do?

2432. Who is the most domineering person I know?

2433. Have I ever eaten rabbit? If not, would I want to?

2434. What is the last thing I saw that was very tasteful?

2435. What is usually an afterthought to some people, but not to me?

2436. Have I ever been scammed?

2437. Do I know someone who has been scammed?

2438. What was my favorite cartoon growing up?

2439. How often do I worry about having balance in my life?

2440. What is currently eminent in my life?

2441. Have I ever seen someone conquer their demons? Who was it?

2442. Is there someone I would like to see conquer their demons?

2443. Where was the last place I visited?

2444. Have I ever ridden a train?

2445. How far have I traveled on a train?

2446. What do I consider to be overrated?

2447. What was the last thing I polished?

2448. When was the last time I was elated over something?

2449. Have I ever played volleyball? Was I good at it?

2450. What part of the day am I most energetic?

2451. Would I prefer being stuck in an elevator or stuck on underground train?

2452. Has something ever left me bewildered?

2453. What was the last wedding I went to that made me laugh and cry? Why?

2454. What is the most remarkable transformation I've ever seen?

2455. Would I be able to live in a place where it rains all the time?

2456. Has there been a place that I have visited that made me feel like I was at home?

2457. In a good cop/bad cop scenario, which would I pick to be? Why?

2458. Who is my favorite interviewer?

2459. What is the ugliest thing I've ever seen?

2460. Have I ever had a limp? What was going on?

2461. What's the one thing I need to do when I'm traveling?

2462. Has someone admitted to me that they are lonely? What did I say?

2463. When the word "whimsical" comes to mind who or what do I think about?

2464. What is the last thing that made my eyes misty?

2465. Have I ever called someone useless?

2466. Have I ever compared oranges to apples?

2467. What's the last thing I boiled water for?

2468. Have I ever witnessed callous behavior from someone unexpectedly?

2469. Have I ever been impressed by someone's determination?

2470. What's a mundane look like for me? Do I experience many of those?

2471. When was the last time I thought something was annoying?

2472. When was the last time I thought someone was annoying?

2473. What is a rare feeling I've experienced?

2474. Who is the gentlest person I know?

2475. Sweet or savory?

2476. Wine, liquor, or beer?

2477. When was the last time I thought I was going to freeze?

2478. When was the last time I thought I was going to melt?

2479. If wanted to get something awful off my chest, who can I always count on to hear me out and never judge me?

2480. When was the last time I was jumpy?

2481. When was the last time someone scared me as a joke?

2482. When was the last time I scared someone as a joke?

2483. Is there a color that can alter my mood?

2484. Have I ever longed for someone? Who?

2485. Have I ever longed for something? What?

2486. What's my favorite snack in an assorted party mix?

2487. What is the one food I always pick out of a dish?

2488. When is the last time I was sore?

2489. When was the last time I was hesitant? Why?

2490. Who is the neatest person I know? Is it me?

2491. When was the last time I was afraid of something?

2492. Have I learned how to navigate failure?

2493. What do I consider to be a failure that no one can recover from?

2494. When's the last time I had to get over someone?

2495. Have I ever been a burden to someone? How did I find out?

2496. What's the last thing I think about before I go to sleep?

2497. What's my bed time ritual?

2498. What do I usually go for when it comes to spice? Mild, medium, or hot?

2499. Is there anyone I know that I would describe as panicky?

2500. Is there anyone I know that I would describe as uptight?

2501. Is there anyone I know who might describe me as uptight?

2502. Have I ever heard important news from second-hand source? How did that make me feel?

2503. What was the last time I swept?

2504. When was the last time I mopped?

2505. What is the one thing I have tried and will never do again?

2506. Has someone been impolite to me recently? What happened?

2507. What's my vision for the future?

2508. What's been the most mature thing I've ever done?

2509. Have I ever been jaded about something? How did I overcome it?

2510. Have I ever bitten into a piece of rotten fruit? Where was I?

2511. When is the last time I saw someone chew with their mouth open?

2512. Who is the last person I waved hello to?

2513. If I magically became a great woodworker, what is the first piece of furniture I would build?

2514. If I magically became a great singer, which singer would I want to duet with?

2515. What have I always wanted to hear from someone? Who is it?

2516. When was the last time I squeezed someone's hand?

2517. When was the last time I held someone's hand?

2518. When is the last time I ever got on a swing?

2519. Have I ever hand washed an article of clothing?

2520. Have I ever hung my clothes to dry on a clothing line?

2521. When was the last time I took a really cold shower?

2522. Do I know how to start a camp fire?

2523. Have I ever screamed at the television?

2524. Have I ever had trouble breathing? What was happening?

2525. When have I not believed in myself?

2526. When was the last time I had a raspberry?

2527. Who do I consider to be legendary?

2528. If my photo was to be hung up in a hall of fame, what would it be for?

2529. Have I ever been distracted by someone?

2530. What does every human in the world need to triumph over?

2531. If I could broadcast a message into every living room in the world, what would it be?

2532. What is the last thing I upgraded in my life?

2533. What's the one thing I wish we could learn from the previous generation?

2534. What makes me want to scream to the high heavens?

2535. What makes me want to give the whole world hugs?

2536. What makes me lose sight of progress?

2537. What reminds me to not lose sight of progress?

2538. When was the last time I was unprepared for something?

2539. When was the last time I was extremely prepared for something?

2540. Who is my favorite actor?

2541. Who is my favorite actress?

2542. Have I ever cracked under pressure?

2543. When was the last time I cancelled on something?

2544. Have I ever crashed a party?

2545. Who do I physically resemble?

2546. Do I have a celebrity doppelgänger?

2547. Have I ever held something back?

2548. What was the last disclaimer I used?

2549. Why is it important for me to use that disclaimer?

2550. When was the last time I had to remind someone to say please and thank you?

2551. Do I tend to make the best of a bad situation? Or do I have to try very hard to do that?

2552. When was the last time I dressed up?

2553. When was the last time I didn't care about what I wore? How did that make me feel?

2554. When was the last time I confessed to something?

2555. Have I ever elbowed someone in a race?

2556. How strong is my mind?

2557. How weak is my mind?

2558. Have I ever tried to solve a Rubik's cube? Was I successful?

2559. Who made me unexpectedly cackle recently?

2560. What is the worst lie anyone could tell?

2561. What is the best lie a person could tell?

2562. When was the last time I was really cranky? Why?

2563. Who is the smartest person in the world?

2564. Is it bad to learn how to be a convincing liar?

2565. What's the difference between a joke and a lie?

2566. Do I usually like to drive straight through to my destination, or do I like making pit stops?

2567. What is the most beautiful scenic road I've been on?

2568. What do I miss about watching live television?

2569. What was the worst part about watching live television?

2570. Roller skates or rollerblades? Why?

2571. What's the best song to roller skate or rollerblade to?

2572. Have I ever wanted something else other than what was in front of me? Did I express that?

2573. Have I ever told someone not to look back?

2574. What is the line between being confident and arrogant?

2575. Do I believe life is simple or complicated?

2576. If I could work from home, would I take it?

2577. Do I believe that one can't ever please everyone?

2578. What do I always reuse?

2579. Have I ever flown a kite?

2580. When was the last time I enjoyed a group outing?

2581. Do I remember an instance when I didn't like hanging out in a large group?

2582. What makes someone an optimal travel companion for me?

2583. Have I ever travelled with someone and never wanted to travel with them again?

2584. Have I recently realized I don't want to spend time with someone anymore? Why?

2585. When was the last time someone shocked me?

2586. What is the last thing I ever customized for myself?

2587. When was the last time something bubbled to the surface?

2588. When was the last time I misunderstood an assignment?

2589. Who do I respect?

2590. Have I ever stuck my tongue out at someone? Why?

2591. Has a cat ever hissed at me?

2592. What was my favorite thing about going to the zoo when I was kid?

2593. Who do I know always thrives under adversity?

2594. Have I ever shaved a part of my body? Why?

2595. When was the last time I took medicine?

2596. What is the one thing I always know how to manage?

2597. Do I know someone who doesn't have one malicious bone in their body?

2598. Have I ever partaken in a survey?

2599. Is there a game show I would totally be great in?

2600. Who is my favorite television host of all-time?

2601. Does world-wide recognition make someone great?

2602. What makes someone a legend?

2603. Have I ever fixed a leak?

2604. Do I know someone who has a hypnotic face?

2605. Do I enjoy fried food?

2606. What is the last thing I wanted to indulge in, but stopped myself?

2607. What insect scares me?

2608. If I was forced to put a price on myself, what price would I choose for myself?

2609. Have I ever been greedy?

2610. What is an odd smell I like?

2611. What's the last thing I touched that was slimy?

2612. What's the last receipt I needed but couldn't find?

2613. Do I tend to keep receipts? Or do I always throw them out?

2614. Washing dishes, do I hate or love it?

2615. Do I know anyone who has been to jail?

2616. Do I know anyone who has been to prison?

2617. Have I ever asked someone about what their experience giving birth was like?

2618. What's the bumpiest ride I've ever been on?

2619. Is there something I consider lethal that most people don't?

2620. Have I ever had a pebble stuck in my shoe?

2621. What is the most inexpensive I own that I treat like is the most expensive?

2622. Do I take care of my physical items?

2623. Has anyone ever accused me of having a bad temper? How did that make me feel?

2624. What's the longest I've gone thinking it was the wrong day?

2625. What is the most nutritious snack I genuinely love?

2626. What is the most nutritious snack that I think taste awful?

2627. Have I ever seen someone get arrested?

2628. Have I ever been in a parade?

2629. What's been the most cumbersome part of my day so far?

2630. When's the last time I was genuinely grateful for the sun?

2631. What's my favorite kind of stew?

2632. What's my favorite kind of soup?

2633. Has someone ever thrown out something of mine by accident?

2634. Have I ever thrown something out by accident that belonged to someone else?

2635. Have I ever wanted to marry anyone?

2636. What's the difference being rich and being wealthy? Which do I want to be?

2637. Have I ever dyed my hair?

2638. When's the last time I cut my nails?

2639. When is the last time I ever had a manicure?

2640. When is the last time I ever had a pedicure?

2641. When is the last time I had a salad? Did I enjoy it?

2642. Is there a restaurant I love because they know my name?

2643. Do I enjoy eggnog?

2644. What is the best imitation I've ever seen?

2645. What were all humans put on this earth to do?

2646. If I had to turn into an element, which would I pick? Why?

2647. If I could combine two animals to describe me, which would they be?

2648. What is the funniest thing I've heard that turned out to be very serious?

2649. Do I laugh when I get nervous?

2650. Who have always had friction with?

2651. Is it my fault I had friction with that person?

2652. Who have I never forgotten?

2653. Who do I know has never forgotten me?

2654. What is the one thing I want my country to change?

2655. What is the one monument I would spend money to go see in person? Why?

2656. Is there any instance where censorship makes sense?

2657. Have I ever been kicked out of a place?

2658. Have I ever kicked someone out of a place?

2659. What's the funniest thing a kid has ever said to me?

2660. What's the saddest thing a kid has ever said to me?

2661. What sound makes me feel safe?

2662. What sound makes me feel unsafe?

2663. Has there been time I was totally cool on the outside but was freaking out on the inside?

2664. If had to come up with a themed restaurant, what would I base it on?

2665. How hard would it be for me to not speak for a whole day?

2666. How hard would it be for me to making a living from being a public speaker?

2667. Do I prefer to drive or walk?

2668. Have I ever called a hotline?

2669. When was the last time someone got me flowers? Did I like them?

2670. What is most powerful, saying hello or saying goodbye?

2671. When is the last time I saw an omen?

2672. If someone put me in charge of all the coffee shops in the world, what would I do?

2673. If someone put me in charge of all the post offices in the world, what would I do?

2674. If someone put me in charge of all the DMVs in the world, what would I do?

2675. If someone put me in charge of all the airports in the world, what would I do?

2676. If someone put me in charge of all the hospitals in the world, what would I do?

2677. Did I like playing Green light/Red light when I was a kid?

2678. What do I consider to be hell on earth?

2679. What's the last thing I heard that made me cringe?

2680. Has anyone called me "honey"? Who was it?

2681. Do I like packing for a trip?

2682. What's one word to describe what it's like to be me?

2683. Have I ever convinced my friends to do something really dumb?

2684. Do I know someone who is a phenomenal father?

2685. What am I allowed to do as an adult that I wasn't a kid?

2686. Have I thought what I would want my funeral to be like?

2687. What am I super chill about?

2688. What am I super high-strung about?

2689. Do I nurture those around me?

2690. What would I name a song about the person who loves me the most?

2691. Have I ever opened an old journal and read it?
What did I learn about myself?

2692. Is there a moment of my life I wish had been videotaped?

2693. Do I feel young?

2694. Do I feel old?

2695. Do I know someone who has gotten ahead in life purely on personality?

2696. Do I believe ignorance is bliss?

2697. Is there something at face value that makes someone seem intelligent?

2698. Is there something at face value that makes someone seem dumb?

2699. What's the last business I saw that surprised me that it was even open?

2700. Do I talk to myself in ways that I would never speak to other people?

2701. What about that status quo frustrates me?

2702. What has shaped my values the most?

2703. Do I believe we can teach people to make better decisions?

2704. What makes a good decision?

2705. What makes a bad decision?

2706. Have I ever been grateful for a conflict?

2707. Do I believe art serves a function?

2708. Do I believe words have power? If so, how much power do they have?

2709. Why do I believe history always repeats itself?

2710. Is looking for personal happiness a selfish act?

2711. Can a perfect society exist?

2712. Have I ever felt like we are living in dystopian society?

2713. What is something that is used for evil but could actually be an agent of good?

2714. When's the last time I sat down to think about the state of the world? How did that make me feel?

2715. What do I contribute to the world?

2716. What do I believe could be the greatest agent for change?

2717. What is the one thing I hear about current events that makes me physically tired?

2718. What is the one large thing everyone in the world can do to change it?

2719. What is the one small thing everyone in the world can do to change it?

2720. What do I think is meaningful change vs. trivial change?

2721. What do I believe would happen if social media was eliminated?

2722. Who do I want to see be braver?

2723. What is my favorite podcast to listen to? Why?

2724. Have I ever met someone who has dealt with addiction?

2725. Why does capitalism get a bad reputation?

2726. What is the power of choice and do I always exercise that power?

2727. What do I think would make our educational system better?

2728. Have I ever flown a drone?

2729. Do I have any scars I am proud of?

2730. Is there a story about that scar?

2731. Do I have any scars I am ashamed of?

2732. Is there a story I can tell about the scar I'm ashamed of?

2733. Is happiness a feeling or an endeavor?

2734. Have I ever seen someone use illness to propel them forward?

2735. When was the last time someone made me feel included? How did it make me feel?

2736. When was the last time a map helped me find myself?

2737. What are my views on morality?

2738. What's a performance that I watch over and over again?

2739. What is a stigma that our society has to do away with?

2740. Who is the best storyteller I know?

2741. Who is the worst storyteller I know?

2742. What do I visualize when I need to find motivation?

2743. What do I visualize when I need to find empathy?

2744. What would happen if there were no more wars?
How would major changes happen?

2745. Do I believe technology has made us connect more with other people or disconnected us from the world even more?

2746. Is there is someone I need to check-in with today?

2747. Dark chocolate or milk chocolate?

2748. What kind of relationship do I have with aging?

2749. How much do I depend on body language when communicating?

2750. What are my views on death?

2751. Have I ever seen a natural disaster that impacted me?

2752. Did I ever have a favorite parent growing up?

2753. What is the best trait I inherited from my dad?

2754. What is the best trait I inherited from my mom?

2755. What is the worst trait I inherited from my dad?

2756. What is the worst trait I inherited from my mom?

2757. When did I realize my parents were normal people?

2758. What is the one thing I definitely want to be different than my parents?

2759. Who have I placed on a pedestal?

2760. Who has placed me on a pedestal? How did that feel?

2761. Who do I revere the most in my life?

2762. Have I ever dreamed of someone that passed away?

2763. What are my views on meditation?

2764. What is my favorite museum?

2765. What is my favorite park?

2766. What is my favorite thing to do when I go to a park?

2767. When I see a full moon, who do I think about?

2768. Who do I believe deserves Nobel prize but has never gotten one?

2769. Is there a book I will most likely always have on my to-read list and never get to?

2770. What belongs in a city?

2771. What doesn't belong in a city?

2772. Do I curse often?

2773. When I was a kid was there something that scared that wasn't that dangerous?

2774. What's the one thing people get wrong about me?

2775. What's a weird thing I notice about someone right out of the gate?

2776. What is the one thing I believe no one can ever look good doing?

2777. Do animals have a personality?

2778. If I could redesign my phone what would I do to it?

2779. Do I have a favorite number? Why has it ended up being my favorite number?

2780. Who was the first musical act I was ever obsessed with?

2781. What is something I've worn that is embarrassing now but when I was wearing it, I felt good?

2782. What's the one app I wish existed but doesn't?

2783. Is there an app that if it didn't exist would make the world severely different than it is today?

2784. What are things I do in my home that are only fun for me?

2785. When was the last time I wanted a job so badly?

2786. What's a great place to go if I had to cry?

2787. Is there a family heirloom I want to have?

2788. What do I believe is the greatest scientific breakthrough?

2789. Who do people consider unattractive that I find stunningly beautiful?

2790. Do I remember when I lost my first tooth?

2791. What was the last insane morning I experienced?

2792. Would I be able to write a book about how to make new friends?

2793. Is there a place I will never go to again?

2794. What I could only say one thing to when I met my personal hero? What would I say?

2795. What is the weirdest hobby I've heard actually exists?

2796. When I turned 21 years old, what was I looking forward to the most?

2797. Did I ever visit a friend at their school? What happened?

2798. If my life was a jukebox musical what would be the opening song?

2799. What have I done to break-up my daily routine?

2800. Have I ever been caught in the middle of a storm? What happened?

2801. What is the one thing I believe my government should do today?

2802. What is something I've tried to understand but just can't wrap my head around it?

2803. What do I want future me to say to present me?

2804. Is there a food I grew to love?

2805. What do I envision to be the best picnic? What would make it great?

2806. What is the most unusual fruit I've ever eaten?

2807. Do I want to be famous?

2808. Is there a time I wish I would have tuned someone out?

2809. What is the one thing I hate about grocery shopping?

2810. What is the list of things I need to be less uptight about?

2811. Is there a cartoon character I should be more like?

2812. The last time I went on a walk, how did I feel?

2813. Is it always good to work hard?

2814. Is there a time working hard doesn't serve a person?

2815. Which do I like going to more, the library or a bookstore?

2816. What is the one mistake I feel everyone has made?

2817. What is the best memory I have of my family?

2818. If I could "freaky Friday" someone, who would I trade places with for one hour?

2819. Who would I trade places with for one day?

2820. Who would I trade places with for one month?

2821. Who would I trade places with for one year?

2822. If I could only have one, would I rather have wealth or health?

2823. Is there a toy from my childhood I have held onto or wanted to hold onto?

2824. What is the funniest thing that has happened to me while I was in the bathroom?

2825. What do I prefer? Bath or shower?

2826. If I were the mayor of where I live, what is the first thing I would do?

2827. What is the one disease I would cure if I could?

2828. What time do I need to go to bed or I just won't function?

2829. What's the worst job I've ever had?

2830. Who was my first celebrity crush?

2831. Would I date someone older or younger? What are the pros and cons of both?

2832. What's something I was never allowed to do as a kid but will definitely let my own children do?

2833. What's my guilty television show pleasure?

2834. Why is it called a guilty pleasure?

2835. What is the worst thing I ever did as a kid?

2836. Is there a secret I will never reveal to anyone?

2837. If I had to change my hair tomorrow, do I go blonde or brunette? Why?

2838. What was a celebrity encounter I've had?

2839. What is currently on my nightstand? Is any of it important to me?

2840. What's the most pain I've ever been in?

2841. If I could have a famous painter do my portrait who would I choose?

2842. What's the last funny movie I watched? Did I like it? Why?

2843. Is there a trend I hope magically disappears?

2844. Is there a song I don't know the words to but sing anyway?

2845. If I were to audition for a talent show, what would be my talent?

2846. What Summer Olympic sport could I watch all the time if I could?

2847. What Winter Olympic sport could I watch all the time if I could?

2848. What were my favorite after-school activities when I was growing up?

2849. What are five things that I find gorgeous in nature?

2850. What have I cried about that when I really thought about it, was just dumb?

2851. When was the last time I felt totally free?

2852. What's the craziest thing I've eaten that I really ended up loving?

2853. What would I do for $100?

2854. Do I tend to travel light or not?

2855. Is there a business I wish would go away?

2856. If there was a house fire what would one thing would I save?

2857. What is the one thing that embarrasses me about my generation?

2858. Is there a company I would never for? Why?

2859. Do I believe in hypnosis?

2860. Has anyone recorded me snoring?

2861. Have I noticed a new way people are entertaining themselves?

2862. What is the main thing I love about neighborhood?

2863. Are my neighbors quiet or loud?

2864. Is there a Halloween costume I wore as a child I would wear as an adult?

2865. Coffee or tea? Why?

2866. How many stamps do I have on my passport?

2867. Have I ever thrown a book out because I thought it was awful?

2868. What is the biggest threat to humankind?

2869. What do I believe is going to be irrelevant very soon?

2870. Have I ever wanted to own a robot?

2871. When I take a break from work, what do I do besides eat lunch?

2872. Is there food I avoid because I have to?

2873. If I never had to see this famous person, I would be super happy? Who is it?

2874. Is there something I was really into that took the world a while to catch up on?

2875. What is the kind of person I attract?

2876. A home-cooked meal or go to a restaurant? Which do I almost always prefer?

2877. When was the last time I experienced road rage?

2878. What did I watch last week that I am still thinking about?

2879. Has there been a moment where I've wanted to freeze people and time?

2880. When was the last time I was in a trampoline?

2881. How young was I when I went on the internet for the first time?

2882. What was my favorite game to play in the playground?

2883. What is television show I don't understand the hype around?

2884. What is the one thing I wish I had learned in school when I was growing up?

2885. How many pairs of shoes do I have?

2886. Is there an annoying habit I just noticed someone has?

2887. When is the last time I found myself annoying?

2888. Have I ever been fired from a job? How did that make me feel?

2889. Is there a movie that manages to always put me to sleep?

2890. Is there a television show that manages to always put me to sleep?

2891. Is internet privacy something I worry about?

2892. What do I prefer more driving or being a passenger?

2893. What is something I know would save me time but no one has invented yet?

2894. Have I ever gambled? Is it something I enjoy doing?

2895. When was the last time I went to casino? What was it like?

2896. Where is the one place all people should volunteer for period of time?

2897. Have I ever witnessed someone littering? How did it make me feel?

2898. What's the funniest thing I've seen on a cake?

2899. Who makes the best cupcakes?

2900. Who do I think is famous right now that will be talked in the next century?

2901. When I go shopping, do I like to go with someone or alone?

2902. What is the one thing I hate shopping for?

2903. If I never had to walk into a store ever again, which store would that be?

2904. What is the worst instance of buying clothes online and it being totally different from what I imagined it would be?

2905. Do I like going to airports?

2906. What do I like most about airports?

2907. What do I dislike most about airports?

2908. What is the longest amount of time I've spent on a plane?

2909. When was the last time my legs fell asleep?

2910. How old should people be when they retire?

2911. What's the weirdest movie I've seen? Why is weird?

2912. What is the worst movie I've seen that ended up not being the worst the second time I saw it?

2913. What is the worst performance I've ever seen in a movie?

2914. What is the best performance I've ever seen someone give in a movie?

2915. What movie would I recast completely?

2916. What television show would I recast completely?

2917. Do I like watching movies with subtitles?

2918. What is the most important thing to happen to me inside a car?

2919. Do I have keys to a house that isn't mine?

2920. Do I have an adoptive family? What are they like?

2921. Who is the most important child in my life? What are they like?

2922. Why is hugging important?

2923. What is the pair of the most comfortable shoes I've ever worn?

2924. When was the last time my bare feet touched the sand?

2925. When was the last time my bare feet touched the grass?

2926. Have I ever been ice skating? What do I like about it?

2927. What's a sport I will never try again?

2928. What is my favorite coffee shop pastry?

2929. When I visit my family, I always have to remind myself of this. What is it?

2930. What was the first hand watch I ever owned?

2931. Why is it important to learn how to tell time?

2932. Flat water or sparkling water? Why?

2933. Have I ever had anything autographed by a celebrity? Why?

2934. When I go to my favorite restaurant, do I always get the same thing? Or do I try different items? Why?

2935. Do I believe I can judge a book by its cover?

2936. Do I have a favorite pillow? Why is it my favorite?

2937. What's the last thing I regret buying?

2938. Have I ever held someone's hand on a first date?

2939. Have I ever killed plant that wasn't mine?

2940. If I had to eliminate breakfast, lunch, or dinner, which would get the chop?

2941. Is there someone I got to when it comes to interior decorating advice?

2942. What is it about a religious cult that attracts people to it?

2943. Have I ever sneaked out of my room when I was young? What would I do?

2944. What is a song I like that is definitely a guilty pleasure?

2945. Is there something that no matter how hard I try not to, I always speak up about?

2946. What do I know today that I did not know last week?

2947. Do I have what most people consider a natural gift?

2948. What is a role I am always happy to fill?

2949. Is there something new I've added to my bucket list? If not, is there something I should add to it?

2950. If I was a car, what kind of car would I be?

2951. What's the best graduation party I've ever been to?

2952. Would I rather eat the same thing I love every day or different things I dislike every day?

2953. Would I rather have more time or more money?

2954. Would I rather eat dinner alone or go to the movie theater alone?

2955. Have I ever been the beneficiary of something? What was it?

2956. What am I constantly evaluating?

2957. When is the last time I sent a good morning text message?

2958. When was the last time I sent a good night text message?

2959. Have I ever been part of a wedding? Did I enjoy the experience?

2960. Is there a former romance I don't talk to anymore, but wish I could?

2961. Has there a moment where I had to check with myself if I was tired or hungry? Which was it?

2962. Who have I ever made a formal complaint about? Why?

2963. When is the last time I ever lit a candle?

2964. Have I ever made a new year's resolution?

2965. How long did I stand by my resolution?

2966. Have I ever worn tight pants? Why?

2967. Have I ever had my teeth whitened?

2968. Have I ever gone spray tanning?

2969. Have I ever gone booth tanning?

2970. Have I ever drunk beer out of a keg?

2971. Have I ever been the designated driver?

2972. What is the worst story I have of being in a cab?

2973. Have I ever car pooled with strangers? What was the worst the part about it?

2974. Have I ever been in love with two people at the same time?

2975. What was something I considered to be the worst thing at the time but then realized years later it wasn't that bad?

2976. What did I think was going to be useless to me as an adult but I ended up using all the time?

2977. If had to be famous, what do I want to be famous for?

2978. What is the one thing I always do when I can't sleep at night?

2979. What would I say is the hardest job in the world? Why?

2980. What would I say is the easiest job in the world? Why?

2981. Is the easiest just as important as the hardest job? Why?

2982. Have my intentions ever been questioned? Why was that?

2983. If I were leading a business team, who are the three famous people I would hire to assist me?

2984. What is the most annoying rhetorical question someone has asked in my presence?

2985. What is the worst filler noise that people use as a crutch when they speak in public?

2986. Who would I wait on head and foot?

2987. Is it true that you can win some and lose some? When has that happened to me?

2988. When was the last time my heart was truly open?

2989. Do I take vitamins? Why? Should I?

2990. Am I a good card player?

2991. What's my favorite card game?

2992. Is there a funny story I can tell about the last time I played cards?

2993. What's the weirdest thing I've seen someone
keep in the trunk of their car?

2994. Do I always carry a tooth brush with me? Why or why not?

2995. Has anyone ever asked upfront if I wanted to be friends with them?

2996. Have I ever asked someone upfront if I could be their friends?

2997. Have I ever called someone a liar to their face? Do I regret doing it?

2998. When have I gained a new perspective on why someone did something
hurtful toward me?

2999. Has anyone ever been angered by my honesty?

3000. Have I ever redeemed myself in the eyes of someone I've respected?

3001. Have I ever crossed a finish line?